Mosquitoes in Paradise

※JOHN R. AURELIO

Mosquitoes in Paradise

※A New Look at Genesis, Jesus, and the Meaning of Life ※

CROSSROAD · NEW YORK

To Emil Ferrucci
of very happy memory

1985
The Crossroad Publishing Company
370 Lexington Avenue, New York, N.Y. 10017

Library of Congress Cataloging in Publication Data
Aurelio, John.
  Mosquitoes in paradise.
  1. Theodicy. 2. Consolation. I. Title.
BT160.A97   1985   231´.8   85-13300
ISBN 0-8245-0698-7 (pbk.)

Contents

Preface

Writing is not like speaking. Over the last five years as the germinal idea for *Mosquitoes in Paradise* took root and grew, increasing numbers of people encouraged me to commit my meditations and speculations to writing. I did so in the hope that there would be food for meditation and spiritual growth here. However, things get lost in the translation. Personalism and simplicity give way to the need to document, footnote, show references, and split theological hairs. It becomes unavoidable since I can't be present in person to answer questions and make distinctions. A transcript of a tape doesn't seem to do it either. Conversation just doesn't translate well into running script. I have tried to make the following text as little pedantic as possible.

In the hope of not burdening the reader with long theological arguments, I have attempted to keep the footnotes and references to a minimum. Furthermore, I have deliberately kept the chapters short so that they can be pondered piece by piece. It is what I call "bite-size theology." You are encouraged to avoid the temptation to read on, novel fashion, until you get to the end. The meal you are about to partake in is new and should be eaten slowly so as to give the system a chance to absorb it without trauma.

Public speakers and writers inevitably must face the his/her/it dilemma. I mean no disservice to the women's rights movement in these pages. The Adam and Eve story in Genesis is a microcosm account of what happens to all of us historically and theologically. (The name Adam itself means mankind.) When I speak of Adam by name and pronoun, I could just as easily, in most instances, substitute Eve. And vice versa. Some authors skirt the issue by using "it." I find that much too impersonal. Until that time when we come up with a new personal pronoun that means him/her, I have opted to use the more traditional method.

Why did I write this book? Over the years in my work with people who are disabled and sick, I have wrestled repeatedly with the question, "Why, God?" In the state institution where I am a chaplain, I've walked through wards of severely handicapped infants and adults, and asked myself, "Why, God?" No less than millions of others who have trod this path before me, I see the innocent suffer and I ask, "Why, God?" I have countless times experienced the joy of healings, some miraculous, but watched the unhealed cry forlornly and wait, and I've asked over and over and over again, "Why, God?"

On the other hand, I have seen the "passed-over" people languish without hope and have heard my God ask, "Why, John?" I have seen relatives and friends of the victims of accidents and disease wrench their hands with despair, and have heard God ask, "Why, John?" I have seen Christians who were put to the test lose faith, and listened to the compassionate God who over the years has heard our plea and given us the answer ask, "Why, John?"

This book was written for all of us who have wrestled with these questions. But it was especially written for the "passed-over" people, those who are in crisis. They need to hear the Good News. Over the years, however, I've learned that the time of the trauma is not always the most effective time to reach them. Once, as a young priest, I was confronted with the accidental death of a young parishoner. Before visiting the funeral home to offer consolation to the grieving parents, I struggled and prayed for some appropriate theological encouragement, a few uplifting scriptural references, some compassionate biblical stories to relate. These I gave to the bereaved parents as best I could at that very difficult time. Several weeks later, when I went to visit them again, I asked if somehow my thoughts had given them some consolation at the funeral parlor. "Oh! Were you there, Father?" they asked. To come in heavy with a Jesus message at the time of trauma may not always be effective. At such a time, consoling presence may be all that's needed. After the shock, when they have time to think apart from the pain, is what this book is for. It is especially for those who are in hospitals, in convalescent homes, who have suffered tragedy. If you think that there is merit in these pages, you might offer them this book as something to read during their unattended moments. Then, pray along with me that they will open their hearts to the working of the Spirit and discover the Good News that's been waiting for them.

Introduction

Has there ever been a time in the life of a Christian when he has not raised a fist to God in frustration and despair and cried out from the depths of his anguish, "Why me, God? Why is this happening to me?" Has this not been the cry of man from time immemorial?

Cain, the son of Adam, pleads with Yahweh, "My punishment is greater than I can bear" (Gen 4:13). The Psalmist cries, "Out of the depths I call to you, O Lord; Lord, hear my cry for help!" (Ps 130). In despair Job curses the day of his birth. "May the day perish when I was born, and the night that told of a boy conceived" (Job 3:3). Even the prophet Jeremiah laments, "Woe is me, my mother, for you have borne me to be a man of strife" (Jer 15:10). Does not Jesus himself confirm that hapless state when he says of Judas, "Better for that man if he had never been born!" (Mk 14:21)?

What we are confronted with here is the age-old problem of evil in the world. Put in other words, "If God is a God of love, then why is there such misery and suffering? Why are there earthquakes, floods, and famines that destroy thousands of innocent people?" Or, what is in reality the ultimate concern, "What did I do to deserve this?"

For centuries mankind has struggled with this problem. Philosophers, theologians, and scholars, as well as ordinary people from every walk of life, have wrestled with it. Countless volumes have been written about it. Yet, the question remains. It will haunt us to the end of time. The solution will continue to evade us until that time "when all things will be made new" (Rev 21:5). All that we can hope to do is to add the insights of this generation to those who came before and cast a little bit more light on what is ultimately a mystery.

That is precisely what the question of evil is, a *mystery*. That means that it can never be fully explained, given our limited intellectual abilities. But this is not reason for despair. Had God not been a God of love, our inadequacy in the face of this Leviathan would easily overwhelm us. However, out of His great condescension, *God has given us the answer to the mystery*. We have the answer, even though we do not comprehend fully the reason for the problem. It is as if we were given the remedy to an incurable illness but we don't know the reason for the sickness. *In the light of the cure the cause fades in significance*. What we must do is to apply the remedy at once. Then we can use the remaining time to inform others of the "good news" and investigate the probable causes so as to avert future tragedies.

This generation is not without its insights. What we must establish first, however, are the ground rules for the investigation.

First of all, we must accept the fact that a mystery can never be fully explained. This means that no explanation will fully satisfy the "all or nothing" inquirer. All we can do is to chip away at the magnitude of the mystery, just as a ray of light can dispel only some of the darkness. What we are called to is faith.

But we must be careful not to relegate faith only to those areas that are beyond the scope of reason. If we do this, as was done all too often in the past, we restrict God to only that which man cannot understand. Then as man's knowledge increases, God's presence decreases. Thus, God would be the God of the ignorant or, conversely, the more intelligent we become, the less need we have for God. To the true believer God is present in all the dimensions of life, the known as well as the unknown. We are asked to trust, to believe, to be faithful even and especially in our pain and darkness.

When General MacArthur left the Phillipine Islands at the time of the Japanese invasion, he promised the people, "I shall return!" The Filipinos believed him and waited, living through the hardships of surrender, occupation and subjugation until he did return and set them free. When Jesus left to go to his Father's house, he promised that he would return in glory. As a faith community we believe him and trust him while we live through pain and suffering until he returns as he said he would, to set us all free.

Secondly, we must accept the fact that there are no easy answers. If there were, they would have been discovered years ago and there would be no need for questions today. Obviously, this is not the case. Unfortunately, this has not deterred the proferring of such simplistic solutions. Without impugning the motives of their authors or demeaning them for their efforts, let us rather examine the inadequacies of these solutions and refrain from using them in the future.

God does not will evil; He permits it. While there is truth in the statement, it is woefully inadequate. It is the type of answer that is designed to get God "off the hook." It would be ludicrous, if it were not so deleterious, to suppose that God would need us to save Him. It would be as if the ant were to defend the elephant. Instead of getting God off the hook, it casts Him in a considerably more negative light. Translating this into the vernacular would be tantamount to saying that a father stands by and watches as his son is being beaten to death, yet apparently does nothing about it. Would his defense, "I did not will it. I merely permitted it," exonerate him in the eyes of others? One would hardly consider this an adequate, let alone a plausible, explanation.

God lets evil happen for some good reason known to Him. On the face of it, this too may seem to be a satisfying explanation. After all, a father, on occasion, will punish a child to teach him a lesson for his own good. Even scripture tells us that to spare the rod is to spoil the child (Prov 13:24). But carried to the extremes which one witnesses every day and God becomes an insensitive ogre. Would a father maim, scar, or cripple a child to make a point?

Sickness and pain are the work of the devil. Causality here is not ascribed to God, as may be in the previous case, but to the devil. On the surface this appears to be a safer argument— inoffensive and less threatening to God. God is not punishing, the devil is. However, this makes the devil as powerful as, if not more powerful than, God, who seems helpless to stop him except in a few rare cases when miracles occur. This conclusion is un-avoidable since sickness—the work of the devil—is far more fre-quent than miracles—the work of God.

There but for the grace of God go I. While on the surface this may not seem to be an explanation for sickness and disability, it is precisely that! What it is stating is that the afflicted one is in such a sorry state because the grace of God was lacking. Pious-sounding phrases, at times, are not only demeaning but theo-logically horrendous. Could one apply that statement to the suffering Christ? That might be a good yardstick with which to measure all future assertions about the theological causes of sickness and suffering.

Reflection

"I am a good person! Why is this happening to me?"

Why do bad things happen to good people? Why do bad peo-ple prosper and good ones suffer? Is there a Christian answer to this age-old problem?

If God is a God of love and justice, where is the love? Where is the justice? Why are some people born healthy and others handi-capped? Where is the justice? Why are some enjoying good health while others bear terrible sicknesses? Where is the justice? Why is it some live long lives and others are cut down in their youth? Where is the justice?

I suppose it is no consolation to know that the wicked also suf-fer, and although there are no statistics to prove it, probably in no fewer numbers than the just. But that is not the issue here. Where is justice when good people suffer?

The answer to this is unavoidably bound up with the account of the fall of Adam and Eve in the garden of paradise. As remote as that may seem to us, as far-fetched as it may at first appear, it is essential to understanding the problem, and it is no more distant to us than today is. If that is where sickness and death began, then we must go back to the cause in order to explain the nature of the disease and to discover its cure. If the diagnosis of a disease is wrong, then the treatment will prove faulty. If in our diagnosis of this problem, this question of justice is incorrect, then our remedies will leave us frustrated. We must go to the cause to determine the cure!

Prayer

Lord! My pain is now and my frustration is intense. Help me to be patient. Help me to see and to understand. And what I cannot know, I pray, then, for an increase in faith.

✴ PART I

The Problem
with Sickness

Bethzatha

The pain in his lower back was worse today so he cursed. It seemed now that there was hardly ever any respite from the pain. With one arm slung over the shoulder of the man carrying him and his legs dragging uselessly beneath him, they carved a tortured path through the sick bodies strewn everywhere beneath the porches.

"Find me a place out of the sun, you jackass!" he screamed as he was being lowered to the earthen floor. His carrier pulled him by the armpits just barely out of the sunlight and dumped him there. "Be back before the sun is fully down or I'll see to it that my father gives you pig's dung instead of a shekel." The man made an obscene gesture which the prostrate man could not see. He threw the sick man's mat down to him. Then walking away, he scratched his behind. That he can see, he thought angrily.

The sick man pulled himself together as best he could. This was another day in an endless succession of days of pain, hopelessness, and boredom. He had grown accustomed to the stench of the unclean bodies around him, but the day had been unusually hot and his absence during the midday heat had cleared his nostrils. It assailed him and taunted him now as if it were an extension of his infirmity, ever there, always waiting for him. Again he cursed under his breath, not because he didn't want the others to hear him as his would merely be just another invective in a vast chorus of grumblings. It was more so because of the futility of it all. It just wasn't worth the effort.

He could no longer recall when it had begun — the crippling. It seemed as if it had been with him all his life. At any rate it had started sometime in his youth. The physicians had applied their remedies but to no avail. Then when these charlatans could do nothing more, could extort no more money from his merchant father, they exonerated themselves by referring them to the rabbis. He had fared no better there. "It is the punishment of God for sin!" What sin could a young man be guilty of to require so terrible a penalty? "If not the sin of the child, then, it is the sin of the father!" It was true that his father was not the most honest of merchants, but then who was? So the guilt was laid upon his father's shoulders and he paid the toll over these many years.

The heat from the sun seemed remorseless today. Even the pool some twenty feet away appeared warm and stagnant. The others kept their distance from him. He was disliked for his wealth that could provide him with litter bearers and for his temperament that voiced loudly his displeasure and disdain of the sickly lot. Why, then, did he come here? As wretched and as smelly as the place was, the pool at Bethzatha offered hope. When the waters of the pool were stirred, the first one to enter would miraculously be healed. He had come close once, only once, to being first. One never knew when it would happen. He had kept a helper with him in those early days of waiting. They had arrived early in the day hoping to get a place as close as possible to the water. The sick who had no other place to go and stayed the night were still asleep. They had just passed the pool when they heard the rush of water behind them. They turned quickly and bumped into an arthritic old man who was on his way to relieve himself. The encounter toppled him directly into the water. He struggled for a while, but then straightened himself out and emerged healed. The old man screamed with delight. He thanked the two of them profusely for the happy accident and hurried away never to be seen again. His own response was to cuff his helper on the back of his head and send him packing. He had never come close again.

He shifted restlessly trying to get more comfortable. A crowd was entering the area, causing a little commotion. It was a rabbi and his peripatetic school. It was not common for visitors to approach this place, let alone learned scholars. The sick were considered unclean and therefore to be avoided. Yet, here was one of some stature, judging from his following. They treaded their way through the prone and seated bodies, deeply engaged in some learning. Perhaps this is Gamaliel, the scholarly and much-venerated rabbi, he thought. Here was a man of distinction and rank whom even he held in esteem.

They made their way slowly through the crowd. When they reached the paralytic, they stopped. The teacher looked down at him. There was a strange, perceptive look on his tired face. Now that he was close, he saw that he was too young to be the great man. Before he could adjust his sentiments, the rabbi addressed him.

"Do you want to be well again?"

"Sir," replied the sick man, "I have no one to put me into the pool when the water is disturbed; and while I am still on the way, someone else gets there before me."

Jesus said, "Get up, pick up your mat, and walk."

He was cured at once, and he picked up his mat and walked away. He could not believe his good fortune. He hurried off without so much a glance back. It was over and good riddance to it. He was free—free at last!

*   *   *

Now that he was free of his crippling sickness, he wasn't sure what exactly he wanted to do. He pushed his way through the startled spectators, struggling to get as far away from the pool and its painful memories as he could. Others were waiting outside. They had seen the miracle and wanted him to talk about it. But he would have none of it. He must get away. There would be time enough later to discuss it. He decided to go home and show his father that the price for the merchant's misdeed had finally been paid. And there was the aide who had dumped him so unceremoniously not an hour before. Would he ever be surprised! He'll be even more surprised when I see to it that he's fired, he thought.

He didn't notice that two priests had broken away from the crowd and were following him. When he was some distance away from Bethzatha, they overtook him.

"It is the Sabbath; you are not allowed to carry your sleeping mat," one of them said.

The paralytic was startled by the accusation. Rolled up under his arm was the mat. He had not given it a thought, let alone that it was the Sabbath. Here was trouble again without his having had time to enjoy his new freedom. Why should he have to pay the price again for someone else's misdeed? He was simply doing what the rabbi had said.

"The man who cured me told me, 'Pick up your mat and walk.'"

They asked him, "Who is this man who said to you, 'Pick up your mat and walk?'"

He cursed and told them that he had no idea who it was. Some teacher, he supposed.

"A false teacher," they quickly corrected. "Only a false teacher would command you to do manual labor which is forbidden on the Sabbath. You had better come with us to report this."

The paralytic protested his innocence all the way to the Temple. Curse the luck that would get me into trouble so soon after my good fortune, he thought. And curse my father whose sin got me into this predicament in the first place.

He had been questioned carefully with a scribe present recording exactly what he said. There was more afoot here than was apparent to him; otherwise why had they spent so much time questioning him about the Messiah. What did they expect him to know of their political wranglings when he had spent most of his life as an invalid? Instinct told him to be wary of these powerful men and fear told him that he had better cooperate or his restored life would be as pitiful as his invalided one.

"If you should remember more or learn more about this false

teacher, you had better report it to us or you will be in even greater trouble. Remember, we have spies everywhere and if we learn that you have been seen with him or have joined his band, we will extract the full penalty for your breaking the Sabbath law."

He thanked them, a bit too profusely, for their leniency and hurried out into the courtyard. He was having more excitement in this one afternoon than he could ever remember. He didn't know what to make of it all. He walked pensively past Solomon's porticoes, still deeply shaken by his brusque encounter with the temple officials. He stumbled right into Jesus.

"Now that you are well again," Jesus said, "Be sure not to sin any more, or something worse may happen to you." That's all he said. Nothing more. Then he and his disciples continued on their way.

The paralytic was now shaking from his head to his feet. Who was this strange man? Why was he doing this to him? He looked around at the crowd gathering beneath one of the porches to listen to him. Surely, one of the temple spies had seen the encounter. Now they would think, beyond a doubt, that he is one of them. Why must he suffer this way? And what did this rabbi mean when he said, "Sin no more"? What sin had he committed? He was innocent of any sin that had caused his crippling condition. Had not the rabbis told him that it was his father's sin? If this man had been a true prophet, he would have known that. Yet, he healed him.

He approached the crowd. "Who is he?" he asked.

"Jesus, a teacher from Nazareth."

He had once heard of him. Among the sick one always hears of healers. He had decided then to stick with what was certain, the healing power of the pool of Bethzatha, rather than go off chasing after spurious healers. He might have thought differently now after what had happened to him, but he caught sight of one of the priests who had questioned him. He had better stick with what was certain. He went back and reported that it was Jesus who had cured him.

Jesus the Healer

What you may have missed in the retelling of the story of the cure at the pool of Bethzatha was that Jesus had to tread his way through numbers of sick people in order to reach the paralytic. To quote John directly: "Now at the Sheep Pool in Jerusalem there is a building, called Bethzatha in Hebrew, consisting of five porticoes; and under these were crowds of sick people — blind, lame, paralyzed" (Jn 5:2-3). And even if he didn't, if the man were perchance on the fringe of the crowd, Jesus could not have been unaware of the others who were lying all about. Yet, the account tells us that Jesus healed only one of them!

What could possibly be the reason for such seeming indifference? Over the years I have heard and read numerous explanations, but they never seemed quite adequate.

• Jesus came to do the will of his Father and the Father told him to cure only one. So, that's all he did.

Considering all the cures that Jesus performed in his ministry, why, in this of all places, would he be restricted to only one cure?

• It was enough for Jesus to manifest his power and it only took one to do that.

The same could be said for other occasions, but the gospel accounts tell us that as many as came to him, he cured them all (cf. Mt 12:15; Mt 14:14; Mt 14:34).

• Jesus did cure others. This account simply doesn't go into all of them.

Why not here when they do so elsewhere? By not doing so, it makes Jesus appear indifferent, if not callous.

• Jesus was in Jerusalem and wanted to keep a low profile.

Healing the sick was not a life-threatening aspect of his ministry. Claiming to forgive sins definitely was (cf. Mt 9:2). Linking the paralytic's illness with sin was sure to draw the attention of the Temple officials who were undoubtedly observing him.

• The question is a moot one. It is a call to faith.

All of Jesus' miracles were a call to faith. Since Jesus was obviously a teacher (rabbi), why should we leave this incident without explanation?

Consider, if you will, that you had the power to heal as Jesus did. Would you not have healed every one of them? Would you walk away from all those outstretched hands after healing only one person? Why did he do it?

Jesus was certainly not indifferent to the plight of the sick. Even after a strenuous day of teaching and healing, Jesus and the disciples got into a boat to get away for a rest. "But the people saw them going and many could guess where; and from every town they all hurried to the place on foot and reached it before them. So as he stepped ashore he saw a large crowd; and he took pity on them" (Mk 6:33-34). A similar incident takes place after the death of John the Baptist. "When Jesus received this news he withdrew by boat to a lonely place where they could be by themselves. But the people heard of this and, leaving the towns, went after him on foot. So as he stepped ashore he saw a large crowd; and he took pity on them and healed their sick" (Mt 14: 13-14). There is no question of Jesus' compassion for the sick. Yet, at Bethzatha he walks into their midst to heal only one of them. After the incident, I'm certain his disciples must have questioned him about this. How could they not have? Unless they already knew and understood the deeper reason behind what Jesus was about. Then that must be what we must come to understand.

Reflection

We are an army. We are beyond counting. We are the sick and the suffering. We lay in wards in hospital factories, a number on a chart to teams of technicians that poke us, probe us, and scare us to death. We waste away in abandoned tenements, on park benches, on subway gratings waiting for the heat of a passing train, because we are human waste. We hobble, we squint, we strain to hear, we cry, we despair. We are guilty and we are innocent. We are wealthy and poor and everything in between. We have cancer, heart disease, cerebral palsy, muscular dystrophy, emphysema, arthritis, syphilis, and a host of other conditions almost as vast and as diversified as we are. We are everyplace and everywhere. We are saints and we are sinners.

We all have this in common — we want to live! We want to be healthy and enjoy a good life. We need to be healed. We are under the five porches waiting.

Prayer

Out of the depths I cry to you, O Lord. Lord, hear my voice.

We lie here waiting for the waters to be stirred, waiting for a cure, but no one knows when that will happen. Will the next doctor who touches me be Jesus? Will the next passer-by be him or a cop telling me to move on? If he comes, I won't be able to see him, or hear him or even walk over to him. Will he pass me by because of all the others? O God, there are so many others here with me. Do you see me? Can you hear me? I am crying to you from the depths of my agony. It is your very own child who cries to you.

Father! Everything is possible for you. Take this cup away from me.

Sickness and Sin

On more than one occasion Jesus links sickness with one's personal sins. He told the paralytic at the pool of Bethzatha, "Sin no more, lest something worse happen to you" (Jn 5:14). On another occasion, a paralyzed man is lowered through the roof in order to reach Jesus. Jesus tells him, "Courage, my child, your sins are forgiven" (Mt 9:2).

The Old Testament psalmist acknowledges this same truth when he cries out, "There is no health in my bones, because of my sin" (Ps 38:3). In Psalm 107 he describes the condition even further. "Some were sick on account of their sins, made miserable by their own guilt, and finding all food repugnant, were nearly at death's door" (vv. 15-16).

All of us are aware that in many cases our own sins lead to our physical and mental disabilities. The terrible hangover after a night of overindulgence leaves no question as to the cause. Venereal disease resulting from promiscuity is one's own accuser. Gastritis from overeating is expected. There is even a growing body of medical evidence that links many physical ailments from arthritis to ulcers with resentment, anger, and the unwillingness to forgive.

Then, there is a whole range of emotional problems that are engendered by sin — the stress of an adulterous relationship; the fear that follows lying; the pressure caused by cheating or stealing; guilt for not doing what one should do, and so on. This is what the psalmist means when in torment he confesses, "My sin is always before me" (Ps 50).

In such cases it is indisputable that healing begins with the renunciation of sin. One cannot be cured of cirrhosis if one continues to drink immoderately; of guilt if one continues to cheat or lie. The ancient proverb puts it bluntly: "As a dog returns to its vomit, so a fool returns to his folly" (Pv 26:11). This is the timeless wisdom Jesus expressed when he said time and again, "Go and sin no more."

Reflection

There is a strong tendency in our time to remove guilt from the world. This is due in great part to the advent of psychiatry. We don't want to lay a guilt trip on people. This is good and I would most heartily concur with it.

There may be a question, however, about what we do to remove the guilt. If one has done nothing wrong, yet feels guilty, then sensitive, compassionate counseling is called for. But if one has done wrong, then the guilt is real and it serves as a call to conversion. To minimize the fault or try to eliminate it entirely is questionable both psychologically and theologically. It must be placed in its proper perspective and dealt with accordingly.

The sinner knows his sin. He must also know that God stands ready to forgive his sin — any sin! Therein lie our true hope and healing.

Prayer

Happy the man whose fault is forgiven,
whose sin is blotted out;
happy the man whom Yahweh
accuses of no guilt,
whose spirit is incapable of deceit!

All the time I kept silent, my bones were wasting away
with groans, day in, day out;

day and night your hand
lay heavy upon me;
my heart grew parched as stubble
in summer drought.

At last I admitted to you I had sinned;
no longer concealing my guilt,
I said, "I will go to Yahweh
and confess my fault."
And you, you have forgiven the wrong I did,
have pardoned my sin.

That is why each of your servants prays to you
in time of trouble;
even if the floods come rushing down,
they will never reach him.
You are a hiding place for me,
you guard me when in trouble,
you surround me with songs of deliverance.

Psalm 32

Sin and the Community

Someone once confessed to me that he stole something. I asked if he wouldn't mind talking about it a little further in order to help me counsel him. He consented and then told me that he had taken a hammer from the factory where he worked. Since the factory ordered such tools in lot consignments, he estimated its value at about a dollar. Certainly not a serious theft but, nonetheless, one with implications beyond what he was prepared for.

He confirmed my suspicions when he told me that everybody was doing it. I informed him that I had recently read an article in the newspaper that thefts at this particular steel mill averaged out to a thousand dollars a week. His hammer along with what others were taking was costing the company over $50,000 a year. "In order to make up for that loss," I told him, "the factory raises the price of steel." Consequently, everyone who bought a car, purchased an appliance, remodeled his house, etc., etc., had to pay the price for his hammer. "You didn't hurt the company," I assured him, "You hurt everybody in this city." After he settled down from the shock, we talked about the social implications of sin.

When John Dunne said, "No man is an island," he was expressing not just a sociological fact by a theological one. Before God there is no such thing as a private sin. Everything we do affects everyone else. This is what St. Paul was talking about when he said, "We are all members of one body. If one part is hurt, all parts are hurt with it. If one part is given special honor, all parts enjoy it" (1 Cor 12:26). Even a sin which apparently has nothing to do with anybody else, weakens the sinner and, therefore, weakens the whole body, the Church.

Science has made this fact demonstrable. When we pollute the environment in one part of the country, the jet stream carries that pollution to other parts of the world. Consequently, trees in Maine are dying from acid rain caused by industrial plants in the Midwest; whales in the South Atlantic are diseased because of refuse from factories in Europe. For the sake of economy, we use chemicals in food that are known to cause cancer; we destroy surplus crops when people in other parts of the world are starving to death. The list is interminable, the facts indisputable. We are our brother's keeper.

We are left with the inescapable conclusion that most of the suffering in this world is the result of sin, our own or others. Therefore, to eliminate all this physical and mental suffering for which we are directly responsible, we must get everyone, everywhere to stop sinning!

Even if this were possible, it still would not account for all suffering. When presented with a man born blind, Jesus was asked, "Rabbi, who sinned, this man or his parents, for him to have been born blind? 'Neither he nor his parents sinned,' Jesus answered" (Jn 9:2). The sin of man can account for most suffering, but not all of it.

Reflection

If we are one with all mankind in the flesh, and if we are all one in the same spirit, then it is inevitable that everything we do affects everyone else. Here we could very well stand in judgment by certain behavioral psychologists for laying a monumental guilt trip on everyone in the world. What are we to do then? Deny the evidence of scripture? Dismiss the intention of God?

Or should we look at this in a positive light? St. Paul says, "No one ever hates his own body, but he feeds it and looks after it"

(Eph 5:29). If we were to see ourselves truly as one body, then we would not do anything to harm one another any more than we would ourselves. Imagine if the whole world were to act in this way!

But we do not see clearly. We see as in a dim mirror, in a confused way (1 Cor 13:12). We sin and hurt one another. The effect is there even if the intention is not. To bring about true reconciliation, justice demands that we seek forgiveness from all those we have hurt. This would be patently impossible for us. But not for God. The God who joins us is the one who restores us. In him is justice rendered and healing effected. When God forgives me, I am healed and so too are all those who accept his forgiveness.

Prayer

Lord, forgive us our trespasses as we forgive those who trespass against us!

The Kingdom of God Is at Hand

> *"Then the disciples went up to him and asked, 'Why do you talk to them in parables?' 'Because,' he replied, 'the mysteries of the kingdom of heaven are revealed to you, but they are not revealed to them.'"* (Mt 13:10)

One of the more fundamental mysteries is the kingdom of heaven itself. It was at the very heart of the message of John the Baptist. "Repent for the kingdom of heaven is at hand" (Mt 3:2). Jesus began his public ministry with the same message. "From that moment Jesus began his preaching with the message, 'Repent, for the kingdom of heaven is at hand'" (Mt 4:17). Jesus sent his disciples out with the same message: "And as you go proclaim that the kingdom of heaven is at hand" (Mt 10:6).

If the kingdom of heaven was at hand in their time, could we still be waiting for it 2,000 years later? That would require some stretch of the imagination for "at hand." ("Close at hand" is the Jerusalem Bible's translation.)

The very context of the biblical passages is that the kingdom of heaven is a now reality. It was present and attainable immediately. "Since John the Baptist came," Jesus says, "up to the present time, the kingdom of heaven has been subjected to violence and the violent are taking it by storm" (Mt 11:12). In the beatitudes, Jesus teaches, "Blessed are the poor in spirit, theirs is the kingdom of heaven" (Mt 5:3).

The kingdom of heaven is not something one has to wait for like the second coming of Jesus. It is present now for those who desire it, who are open to it, who have the faith to see it. "The reason I talk to them in parables is that they look without seeing and listen without hearing or understanding. . . . But happy are your eyes because they see, your ears because they hear! I tell you solemnly, many prophets and holy men longed to see what you see, and never saw it; to hear what you hear and never heard it" (Mt 13:13-17).

What, then, is the kingdom of heaven that they were privy to? Responding to the prophecy of Isaiah, Jesus sends the disciples of John back to him with this message, "Go back and tell John what you hear and see; the blind see again, the lame walk, lepers are cleansed, and the deaf hear, and the dead are raised to life and the Good News is proclaimed to the poor; and happy is the man who does not lose faith in me" (Mt 11:4-5).

There is no question that the healing of sick people was a sign of the presence of the kingdom. So, too, was the raising of the dead. But that was not all of it. They were the works that gave testimony to Jesus. When confronted about blasphemy, Jesus defends himself by appealing to his works: "Then even if you refuse to believe in me, at least believe in the work I do" (Jn 10:38). Belief in Jesus is more important than the works he performed! They were "signs," as John referred to them, and as signs they pointed. That is the purpose of a sign. They were signs of the kingdom, but not the kingdom itself.

So, too, is the poor having the Good News preached to them a sign of the kingdom of heaven. We can readily understand the other signs, bodies made whole again, the dead restored to life; but what is the Good News? Was this not the preaching of Jesus? Was this not what so many onlookers saw and heard, but did not understand? If miracles and healings were all that were needed to enter the kingdom of heaven, then that would have been enough for Jesus' ministry. In that case, just seeing and accepting a paralytic man walk, or hearing and accepting a mute man speak, would have been enough to gain entrance to it. Or it would have been enough to just ask for and receive a healing. But that was not enough. Neither is it today!

Neither is it enough to have the Good News preached to you. That, too, is a sign of the kingdom. Its purpose is to point, in the same way as the other signs. Otherwise, just hearing the Good News would be sufficient to gain entrance. It did not in Jesus' time, and it does not now.

Nor is it enough simply to appeal to Jesus. "It is not those who say to me, 'Lord, Lord,' who will enter the kingdom of heaven, but the person who does the will of my Father in heaven. When the day comes many will say to me, 'Lord, Lord, did we not prophesy in your name, cast out demons in your name, work many miracles in your name?' Then I shall tell them to their faces; I have never known you; away from me, you evil men!" (Mt 7:21-23).

Once again we are left with the question, "What is the kingdom of heaven?" If the signs simply point to it, then they themselves are not the kingdom. The signs Jesus performed pointed to him (Jn 10:38). In him is the kingdom of heaven. There can be no other answer. If we "put on the Lord Jesus Christ" (Rom 13:14), that kingdom is attainable by us now as it was to those who were present to him then.

And the mysteries of that kingdom are revealed by him to those who have faith in him. We must enter into Jesus so that we will see as he sees and understand as he understands. In Jesus, the kingdom of God is at hand!

Reflection

When the great man of letters G. K. Chesterton faced the criticism that Christianity has failed, his answer was that it hadn't been tried yet. That answer is, at first sight, a clever rejoinder. Unfortunately, it is not a liveable solution, one you can live with over the long haul. One could then say that if it hasn't been tried over all these years, it has failed the test of time. It's time to try something else.

But it hasn't failed the test of time. Christianity is still with us and is still flourishing. What is the answer to this great paradox?

Jesus gives us the answer. The kingdom of heaven is like a mustard seed. It is the smallest of all the seeds, but grows into one of the largest of trees (Mt 13:31). It is true for the church and it is true for the individual.

It is the seed planted in us in baptism. There are days in our lives when that kingdom radiates through us. We feel good. We are in tune with God. We illumine the lives of all those we touch. All is well with us and the world.

But there are times of darkness, times of aridity. Branches of our lives wither and become brittle. There is no warmth or shelter for birds amid the sparse leaves that give fading evidence of life.

Still, there is hope. The gardener will come at our call to prune away all that hinders growth and starves life. We will be made new again, vibrant with leaves, radiant with blossoms, overflowing with life. The tree, the kingdom, is eternal!

Prayer

Lord Jesus, the kingdom of heaven is within me and about me. When it is weak within, let the kingdom without nourish and sustain me. When it is weak without, let my strength replenish it. You are the vine and we are the branches. In you, we are eternal!

✳ PART II

There's Trouble in Paradise

Mosquitoes in Paradise

What was it like in Paradise before the sin of Adam? I can remember back to my childhood being taught that it was an idyllic place, a sort of primitive fantasy island. It was a wonderland where our first parents never suffered; where Adam never had a stomach ache or Eve a headache, where the weather was always balmy, and man all but talked to the animals. The very mention of the word "paradise" conjures up all those same notions even today. The question is how true is that image?

There are scriptural and theological reasons that may have led to those conclusions, but there are also scriptural and theological reasons that can lead to other conclusions. The former have a hallowed place in our traditions and are indelibly impressed in our minds, so it is no easy matter to call them into question. The latter have only recently entered into my speculations and meditations. Nonetheless, I believe they bear serious consideration.

In one of his parables Jesus tells about a man who sets out to build a tower. He must first sit down and work out the cost to see if he has enough to complete it. "Otherwise, if he laid the foundation and then found himself unable to finish the work, the onlookers would all start making fun of him" (Lk 14:28). Over the years, we have been building a tower with the understanding that it has a solid foundation and there is sufficient wherewithal to finish the task. The materials we used were for the most part good and durable. The structure rose layer by layer to considerable height. Occasionally, it would unaccountably tremor down to its foundation. Especially when it was under seige. A few good sturdy supports, strategically placed, and the work continued again.

The tower is our scriptural/theological understanding of sickness. The insights of great thinkers over the years have given rise to a mighty structure. When it was under attack, a few well-chosen theological aphorisms, strategically placed, were all that was needed to shore up the structure. But, periodically, strange unaccountable rumblings have been felt down to its very foundations. Especially today with the onslaught of abortion, euthanasia, eugenics, and a whole host of other medical "advances."

How we conceive of the garden of Eden is central to the very foundation of our structure. However, it is extremely important that we bear in mind that prior to the sixteenth century, philosophers and biblical scholars believed on the evidence of scripture that the world was flat; that it rested on two pillars; and that the sun, planet, and stars revolved around the earth. In the light of today's legitimate scientific findings some of our notions of Paradise must appear untenable. Is it possible to claim today that there would have been no earthquakes, volcanic eruptions, violent windstorms in Paradise? Can we reasonably assert that the entire animal and insect world was friendly to man? Or have we come to that stage in the building of the tower where we can go no higher without being laughed at?

I wonder if those idyllic visions of Paradise are essential to the structure, or even necessary? The scriptures themselves make them questionable. What we must do is to take a new look at Paradise.

Reflection

One of the proofs for the existence of God advanced by Thomas Aquinas was the order in the universe. To disprove this theory a college professor dropped a number of spheres in a large container of water. He then stirred the waters in a circular motion and asked the class to notice that none of the spheres collided or touched one another. "This explains your order in the universe," he announced triumphantly. The students were delighted at its simplicity, until one of them asked, "Sir, who stirred the heavenly waters?" "Oh, well! Back to the drawing board," the professor commented wryly.

We must not ascribe to man the things that are God's. Nor must we ascribe to God the things that are man's. History is all too filled with sorry examples of the latter: Caesars, pharaohs, and kings who considered themselves divine; wars fought in the name of religion; perversity sanctioned by the gods. Divine revelation is one thing. What man infers from that is quite another. There are times when we must all go back to the drawing board.

Prayer

Come, Holy Spirit! Fill the hearts of your faithful and enkindle in them the fire of your divine love. Send forth your Spirit and they shall be created. And you shall renew the face of the earth.

God Saw That It Was Good

On the first day of creation God said, "Let there be light, and there was light. God saw that the light was good" (Gen 1:3). On another day, "God called the dry land 'earth' and the mass of waters 'seas,' and God saw that it was good" (Gen 1:10). On the succeeding days God repeats His observation and ends with the same comment—it is good. But on the sixth day, "God said, 'Let the earth produce every kind of living creature' and 'Let us make man in our image.' God saw all He had made, and indeed it was very good" (Gen 1: 24,26,31). It comes as no startling revelation to someone familiar with the Bible that God was pleased with His creation. It was good and even very good.

And that's precisely the point! If something is good, it implies that there is a better. If there is a better, then there must also be a best. The author of Genesis alludes to this when he writes "very good" for the sixth day. He was obviously aware of degrees of good or he would not have made that comment on the sixth day. The unavoidable implication is that if God wanted to, He could have made things better.

I have friends who are forever remodeling things wherever we go. They talk about landscaping yards, redecorating churches, and redesigning whole cities. At times like that, I jokingly tell them how unfortunate it was that they weren't around at creation, because then they could have told God how to do it right. My jest was based on fact. God did not say "very good" on the first day. Nor did He say, "This is the best," on the sixth day. Where things are good, the creative imagination can come up with a better.

The garden Adam was placed in was good, as was the creation that surrounded him. It was not perfect. Adam did not walk around in idyllic leisure. In fact, he had to work. "Yahweh God took the man and settled him in the garden of Eden to cultivate and take care of it" (Gen 2:15). There was no living off the fat of the land for him. He did not while away his hours picking fruit off the trees and napping in the noonday sun. He had to till the soil by hand, which is no simple task as any gardener or farmer can testify. It would be difficult to imagine him doing that without working up a sweat. Furthermore, since he had to "take care of it," could that have meant more than just watering and pruning? Would he have to protect it from foraging animals and insects?

How then did we conceive of Paradise as "the best"? If Adam and Eve were totally happy, then there would be no room for improvement. If there were no problems in Paradise, what did the mosquitoes do?

Reflection

There are days when it is difficult for me to see things as good, let alone better or best. A day of rain may be taken as good. A week of rain is depressing. When I suffer for a short time or when I know that my pain is only temporary, I can endure it with some measure of hope. But, when there is no end in sight, when there is no promise of relief, the agony is unbearable.

Prayer

It is at such times, Lord, that I need your words for encouragement. When pain calls me to myself, you must help me to look outside beyond me. As a child when I felt sick to my stomach, my mother used to tell me to look at the sky. Whenever I did, the queasy feeling eventually went away. Was it meant just to distract me or was it simple wisdom? If I look to your wonderful heavens and the marvelous work of your hands, I cannot help but be struck by the goodness that surrounds me. I see fields of flowers swaying in the summer breeze and my spirit is filled with the beauty you have given me. A silver moon glistening through ice-covered trees; a night emblazened with a million sparkling stars; a solitary bird singing a canticle to the dawning sun — all these are good, Lord. Remind me of them when life seems to have lost its simplicity.

Fill the Earth and Subdue It

> *"God blessed them saying to them, 'Be fruitful, multiply, fill the earth and conquer it'"* (Gen 1:28).

There is a long-standing tradition, based on the scriptures, that death is the result of the sin of Adam. When Eve is questioned by the serpent about eating the fruit, she responds, "God said, 'You must not eat it, nor touch it, under pain of death'" (Gen 3:3). After she and her husband eat the fruit, God enforces the curse, "For dust you are and to dust you shall return" (Gen 3:19). The supposition that rightly follows is that had they not sinned, they would not have died. St. Paul confirms this in his letter to the Romans, "Through one man sin entered the world, and through sin death" (Rom 5:12).

The natural state of man, however, is mortal. Therefore, we must establish from the outset that God is not subject to the laws of nature. The common man, as well as philosophers and theologians, have recognized this for centuries. God can dispense from His own rules. He can stop the sun in its course; He can part the waters of the sea; he can give to mortal man the gift of immortality in the natural state. The name given to this is preternatural gift. Adam and Eve had this gift before original sin. The effect of the sin was to separate man from God. This separation is "death"—spiritual and eternal. Physical death is the symbol of it.

Consider, if you will, if Adam had not sinned and man were

not to die, how long would it have taken this multiplying man to "fill the earth"? Two possibilities come to mind. First, as people increased, the space available to them would necessarily decrease. Consequently, God would have to expand the present world or move the excess number of people to another one. On the other hand, if Adam hadn't sinned but one or the other of his children did (each would have to have his own test, the argument goes) and thereby incurred mortality, then some would be multiplying and living eternally, while others, the mortal ones, would merely slow up the process of filling the earth, but not eliminate it. When one considers the evidence of scripture as to the effects of the fall, the possibility of further complications becomes staggering. Cain murdered his brother in a jealous rage. Could we not assume that the children of the fall would be murderously jealous of those with immortality? Would they attempt to solve the problem of overcrowding in their own way? "O, beata culpa!" St. Bernard sings out about the sin of Adam. "O, happy fault!" because it brought such a wondrous solution, Jesus Christ. In a lesser sense here, we can say "O, happy fault!" because it eliminated the need for some monumental unraveling.

Now, to finish God's statement — "and conquer it." (Other translations use "subdue.") The word "conquer" is a military term referring unmistakably to warfare. Why would one have to conquer a world one is at peace with? Why would one have to struggle against (subdue) a creation one is living in harmony with? Does the statement imply that there were struggles in Paradise, struggles that can aptly be described only in terms of conflict and war? In this conflict, could Adam have broken a leg or Eve sprained an ankle?

Are there possibilities here not yet discussed or explored?

Reflection

I have been told that an eagle teaches its young to fly by urging it out of the security of its nest into the frightening void of space.

The eaglet flaps its untried wings frantically while it falls help-lessly toward the earth. However, before tragedy occurs, the eagle swoops beneath it and bears it up again on its wings.

Life demands an openness of me. I cannot hedge all my bets, no matter how many precautions I take. I want to be sure. I need to be secure. So I plan, struggle, and set up as many safe-guards as I can. Yet, there is still doubt. But if I were to be able to take care of myself totally, I would have no need of God. I would have made myself God.

Prayer

Help me to do my best, Lord. Then, like the eaglet, let me trust you to bear me up when I am falling down.

✳ *Day Nine*

It Is Not Good for Man to Be Alone

"Yahweh God said, 'It is not good that man should be alone. I will make him a helpmate'" (Gen 2:18). The state of Adam being by himself was a condition considered by God as "not good." This would seem to imply two realities: that he was imperfect or, at least, not complete and that he was lonely. Yet how could this be in an idyllic Paradise? The very use of the word "helpmate" implies that in some way the man needed help. This was his condition before he was guilty of sin.

> *"Yahweh God built the rib he had taken from the man into a woman, and brought her to the man. The man exclaimed: 'This at last is bone from my bones, and flesh from my flesh!'"* (**Gen 2:22-23**)

The use of such dramatic words as "exclaimed" and "at last" serves to heighten the presumption that the man was waiting, if not longing, for a woman. If he were totally complete, he would not have needed a helpmate. If he were totally happy, he could have watched all creation pair off and mate without the slightest sense of loss or absence. Indeed, did not Jesus in referring to the resurrection state that at that time there will be no marrying or giving in marriage? They will be like the angels in heaven (Mt 22:30). If that is to be the condition of man in the resurrection, it certainly was not the condition of man in Paradise.

Reflection

Why is it I am so lonely? Why is it there is so much loneliness around me? Even those who are married are not spared.

Everything about me says community. My body is community —the joining of my father and mother is evident throughout me. I belong to a family, a neighborhood, a city, a nation. The world is a community united by a common flesh.

There is a community of spirit about me. I am one with those I laugh with, I cry with, I work with, I suffer with, I triumph with. I am one in spirit with all mankind.

Prayer

Lord, I am lonely. When the laughter fades, when the tears dry, when the neighborhood settles down, when the nation rests, even when the deepest intimacy is over, I am lonely again. It is then that you call me. "For you have created me for yourself and our hearts are restless. But they will not rest until they rest in you" (St. Augustine).

To the Woman

"To the Woman he said, 'I will increase your pains in childbearing'" (Gen 3:16). Other translations use "multiply your pains." In either event, the implication is the same—there was pain! One cannot multiply what is not there. It is a mathematical certainty that zero times a hundred or a million, for that matter, is still zero. If there were no pain in childbearing or otherwise, then God would not have used the word "increase." He would have said, "I will give you pain," or "You will discover pain."

Again, a number of possibilities present themselves. Did our first parents discover the meaning of pain when they sinned and consequently God applied that to the woman in the area that was uniquely hers? But, then, would not "loss" or "anguish" have been a more appropriate word? What she would have experienced in that case would have been the loss of what she had before or the anguish that would result from that loss. The reading should then be, "I will multiply the sense of what you've lost when you bear children." Or another possibility, "I will increase the anguish you now feel, especially when you bear children."

But God did not say "loss" or "anguish." He said pain! Is there an implication in the passage that Eve had already experienced childbirth; that God was increasing what she already knew? However, we know of no children before the fall. If there were no children, yet Eve knew the pain of childbearing, could we possibly presume that she had had a miscarriage?

Or is it more probable to assume that Eve was not ignorant of pain?

Reflection

Pain surrounds me and envelops me. It is a long and constant companion. I seek answers and there are none and my pain is intensified. What have I done to deserve this?

Prayer

In my desperation, I cried out, "Lord, I shall abandon you. I shall look elsewhere for answers."

I went to the world. The world gave me reasons, explanations, theories, and endless possibilities. But it gave me no hope.

I went to the flesh and for a while I forgot. But the pain returned with even greater intensity.

I went to the devil. But he delighted in my anguish.

Lord, to whom shall I go? You have the words of eternal truth. Speak, Lord. Your servant is listening.

The Tree of Knowledge

The vision of Paradise as free of struggle and pain somehow also carried with it the notion that man also had full or near-perfect knowledge. To our dismay as children we were given to understand that if Adam hadn't sinned, there would have been no need to go to school. While his knowledge would not have been perfect (only God has perfect knowledge), it would have been at least angelic or intuitive (perceived by intuition and not by experience). This, perhaps, can be derived from an amplification of God's statement in the garden, "You may eat indeed of all the trees in the garden. Nevertheless of the tree of the knowledge of good and evil you are not to eat" (Gen 2:16). All that Adam saw and knew was good. He had tasted (knowledge) of all the trees in the garden, but he had no experiential knowledge of evil. His knowledge, at least negatively speaking, was limited.

The question arises, however, that if Adam did not have incredible knowledge (near-perfect, intuitive, or otherwise), how could he be guilty of committing so serious a sin? Perhaps that can best be answered by asking another question. If Adam had no knowledge of evil or sin prior to the fall, did he have knowledge of lesser evil or venial sin? (In traditional theology a sin was considered mortal if it brought death to the soul by turning one away from God. Minor infractions which diverted one from the proper course were termed venial.) If he didn't, then he couldn't have been very culpable for choosing something he had absolutely no knowledge of.

If we accept degrees of sin, even venial ones (the term, however, is misleading because theologically it is no sin at all), then Adam would have had some inkling of the magnitude and consequence of his act. How could one be held accountable for choosing total evil when he has no concept of what evil is? A condition for committing mortal sin is that one have "sufficient knowledge" of what one is doing. Ignorance of the law may not excuse in the civil order, but it does in the theological order. One cannot commit sin by mistake or inadvertently.

Adam had the ability to make a moral choice — the choice between right and wrong. After all, he knew what was good and what was not good. It was not good for him to be alone. That he experienced. It was not good to eat a rotten apple. That, too, he experienced. It was not good to taste evil. That he had not experienced. He had to rely on God's judgment in that matter.

In Hebrew, when opposites are linked together, they refer to the totality that exists between them. For example, day and night means all the time; East and West means everywhere; good and evil means everything. When Adam and Eve wanted "to know" good and evil — that "know" meant more than an intellectual understanding of it. It meant a deep, personal relationship (almost sexual, as in Mary's statement, "I do not know man") and commitment to it. Their intent was more than simple disobedience. It was to assume the prerogatives of God. Their sin was a sin against faith because they were asked to rely on the judgment of God. They were capable of mortal sin because they could multiply what they knew as not good to a serious degree.

In other words, Adam and Eve did not have to have "perfect" knowledge in order to commit the original sin. They only needed the limited, though sufficient, knowledge that they possessed. If their knowledge had been perfect, they would never have sinned. It was their desire for perfect knowledge that led to the fall.

Reflection

The mind is a mixed blessing. It is the battleground of sin, the playground of imagination, and the limbo of emotions. It can be the source of our exaltation, as we conquer one unknown after another; and the reason for our capitulation, when we cannot accept our limitations. We use it to delight in possibilities and to stagnate in corruption. It is a Pandora's box of emotions not always subject to the will's demand to impose, compose, or dispose. It is God's jewel and the devil's amulet.

Prayer

O Lord, you have created me in your image; you breathed your spirit into me and gave me life. Teach me your ways. Help me to walk in your paths.

Teach me to love—freely, always—for it is in loving that I resemble you and my mind is at rest.

Teach me to forgive—quickly, unreservedly—for it is in forgiving that my mind is unshackled and I am set free.

Teach me to listen—openly, quietly—for listening is the beginning of wisdom and wisdom is your footstool.

Teach me to follow—obediently, joyfully—for in you I trust and in all your plans for me I am at peace.

Teach me to suffer—humbly, patiently—for through suffering I enter the heart of mystery; in suffering I acknowledge you as Lord; by suffering I am purged, I am redeemed.

You Shall Most Surely Die

To take the words of scripture literally in my other speculations and not to here would be weak if not manipulative. Yet, even the words taken literally seem to indicate more than what is apparent. God says to Adam: "On the day you eat of [the forbidden fruit] you shall most surely die" (Gen 2:17). Why the emphasis—"shall most surely"? I suppose it is safe to assume that not all living creatures were gifted with immortality. Otherwise, how would Adam even know what death is? Then why not simply say, "You will die," or "You will know death"? Why add, "most surely," or "indeed"? Could there be another significance to death about which we have not speculated? Could there have been the possibility of a death which was not as we perceive it today—awful, frightful, negative? Since we really don't know what life was like before the fall, how then do we know what death, even without the gift of immortality, would have been like?

Along with the question of death, one must also consider the question of pain and suffering. Could Adam have suffered? Did he? I suppose when one begins conjecturing about an immortal man, a vision of him having lost an arm, an eye, or a leg, and living forever that way, would seem incongruous if not ghoulish. Of course, that would be in retrospect from our point of view. But is bodily perfection a necessary corrolary to human immortality?

In order to support a theory of bodily perfection one is forced to posit all sorts of bizarre suppositions. Adam could never have tripped and scraped a knee. There could have been no infections or his body would have had to have incredible restorative powers. Subduing the earth could not have occasioned any adverse possibilities. He could never have fallen from a tree or eaten anything that upset him. Such a litany could go on and on, making of Adam more superman than man.

Are we forced to make such assumptions? Must suffering always be perceived as bad? Is suffering a natural consequence of our created finiteness, which even the preternatural gift of immortality did not remove? Pope John Paul II in his letter on "The Christian Meaning of Human Suffering" states that, "suffering seems to be particularly essential to the nature of man."

There is a saying in theology, "grace builds on nature." This means that God does not impose a whole new order on mankind in order to give us His grace. In other words, God uses what we've got (what He's given to us) to build on. For example, God does not expect a tree to sing in order for Him to bless it. Jesus cursed the fig tree because it didn't do what it was supposed to do, what was natural for it to do. God blesses us for doing what comes naturally. It is natural for us to make choices. God blesses us when we make good choices.

Is it not in the natural order of living things to grow, to age, to change, to experience pain? Is it reasonable to assume, therefore, that in the natural order of things all these conditions would have to be revoked, changed, or suspended unless or until man were to sin? So many negatives do tend to confuse the argument. Let's put it positively. God creates man in a natural state and then, immediately, suspends everything having to do with it. We are left to wonder why He created us in that state in the first place. If grace builds on nature, what was left for man to build on? Then, when man sins, God punishes him by restoring him to the way He originally made him. Are we to assume that the natural state of man is a punishment which God held over Adam as a threat against sin? How then can creation be considered good?

If on the other hand the gift of immortality did not remove

man from the natural state, and he was able to experience suffering and pain, what good was Paradise?

Reflection

All living things die. All nonliving things are eternal. What irony! Man dies and stones endure. Intelligence, brilliance, and creativity pass away while inertness, dumbness, and mindlessness perdure.

Animate man worships inanimate things. What foolishness! We build monuments to our envy of them. We raise pyramids of stone that will endure longer than the corruptible flesh that rots within. We hoard wealth that outlasts us and mocks us as it passes from one generation to the next.

The spirit of man that can soar beyond telling is subservient to the body of man that can barely leap beyond its own height. What perversity! We are slaves to the demands of our bodies. We go to any length to feed it, to shape it, to tone it, to exercise it, to pamper it, to paint it, to perfume it, to satisfy it. No one is exempt. Not even the intelligent. (Only the wise.) A physical body with not a cosmic measurable comparison to the potential of the mind makes the greater its slave. If not for wisdom, the world would indeed be a stage of fools.

Prayer

O God, you alone are immortal. There is no immortality save in you! That is wisdom.

Figuratively Speaking

"And if your hand should cause you to sin, cut it off; it is better for you to enter into life crippled, than to have two hands and go to hell, into the fire that cannot be put out. And if your foot should cause you to sin, cut it off; it is better for you to enter into life lame, than to have two feet and be thrown into hell. And if your eye should cause you to sin, tear it out; it is better for you to enter the kingdom of God with one eye, than to have two eyes and be thrown into hell . . . . " (Mk 9:43-47).

Doubtless there are appropriate times when one may look at the words of scripture and take them figuratively. In the above passage Jesus warns the sinner to cut off his hand or foot or eye rather than risk the loss of the kingdom. But, he says, it is better to enter the kingdom of God with one eye than to have two and be thrown into hell. Does this mean that one may be minus an eye in the kingdom of God? Is this to be taken literally or figuratively?

Consider the context. Jesus is speaking pointedly and forcefully. The previous statement in Mark's gospel is about scandalizing children. If one is guilty of this, it would be better for him to have a millstone put around his neck and be cast into the sea. Jesus is certainly not mincing words here. There is a natural repugnance toward anyone who would corrupt children. He would hardly be speaking figuratively.

In Matthew's gospel Jesus makes the same statement in another context. He quotes the old law forbidding adultery. Then he adds, "But I say this to you: if a man looks at a woman lustfully, he has already committed adultery with her in his heart" (Mt 5:27). Then he adds, "if your right eye offends you, pluck it out. . . ." He would certainly seem to be speaking literally, especially considering the audience who were accustomed to taking things literally, an eye for an eye, and a tooth for a tooth.

Furthermore, speaking figuratively when one is attempting to make a strong point only serves to weaken the argument. It would hardly serve Jesus' purpose to have done so in these instances.

Are we to assume, then, if Jesus was speaking literally, that one may be in the kingdom of God without all his faculties? What does that do to our stereotyped images of heaven where bodies are made whole again and everyone is beautiful? But the other side of the question also needs to be asked. "If I will be dashingly handsome when I get to heaven, will it still be me?"

Reflection

I have heard those who suffer terrible physical pain say they would prefer mental problems to physical agony. I have heard those suffering mental anguish plead for physical pain instead. I have seen the poor jealous of the rich and the rich envious of the poor. I have watched the unknown struggle for notoriety and the famous crave anonymity.

"I am what I am," sings Popeye the sailor man. Perhaps it is a comment on our times that wisdom should come from comic strips. It is what we do with what we've got that makes us who we are. After the resurrection, Jesus was recognized by the wounds in his hands and the hole in his side. Would it have been Jesus without them?

Prayer

God, grant me the serenity to accept the things I cannot change; the courage to change the things I can; and the wisdom to know the difference.

Serenity Prayer

But God, grant me the courage not to give up on what I think is right even though I think it is hopeless.

✳ *Day Fourteen*

The Man Born Blind

"As he went along he saw a man who had been blind from birth. His disciples asked him, 'Rabbi, who sinned, this man or his parents, for him to have been born blind?' 'Neither he nor his parents sinned,' Jesus answered" (Jn 9:1-2).

It has been a common teaching that sickness and death are the consequence of sin. Does that mean all sickness? Here, seemingly, is a case that does not apply. Jesus blames neither the man nor his ancestors for the blindness. Is this an exception to the rule? If so, could there have been others like him or did God arbitrarily choose this one innocent man to inflict punishment on so that Jesus could make a point? If the blind man's condition is the result of his own sin, it may be considered in some way as just. Even if it were the result of his ancestors' sins, it would have been considered just, as attested to numerous times in the Old Testament. But to say that God inflicted it without anyone's culpability would be to say that it is unjust.

Could there be a middle ground? Could blindness or any other disability not be considered an evil? In a statement to the crowds at Lourdes on August 15, 1983, Pope John Paul II stated, "Neither just nor unjust, suffering remains, even with partial explanations, difficult to understand and to accept even by those who have faith."* Could there be a way of looking at sickness (and even death) apart from the notion of evil? Is there a hint of this in Jesus' next statement: "Jesus answered, 'he was born blind so

---

*L'Osservatore Romano, September 5, 1983.

that the works of God might be displayed in him.'" What are these "works of God" that God is using this blind man to teach us? Why a blind man?

Reflection

Beethoven wrote his great musical masterpieces when he was deaf. El Greco, the artist, was reputed to have distorted vision. A one-legged man runs a marathon across Canada. An armless woman paints with a brush clenched between her teeth. A certified public accountant keeps books with a pen held by his toes.

Prayer

Alone I can do nothing. With God, there is nothing I cannot do.

A Final Word About Death

In 1 Corinthians 15, St. Paul compares Jesus to Adam, referring to him as the last Adam. This comparison has given rise to continuous speculation by ancient Christian writers, the Fathers of the Church, and theologians down through the centuries in many religious and liturgical texts. It is the source of Jesus' designation as "the second Adam."

Consider Jesus as the second Adam. Since Jesus never sinned, might we not speculate, therefore, that his human condition was the same as that of Adam before the Fall?

Even though we may not separate Jesus' divinity from his humanity, for the two are inextricably intermixed (he was at one and the same time true God and true man), there are times when distinctions are forced upon us. Luke's Gospel tells us that Jesus "grew in wisdom, age and grace" (Lk 2:52). Certainly, not in his divinity. Could there not then be a parallel between the sinless Adam and Jesus, at least in their humanity?

We know that Jesus grew in wisdom, age, and grace. Why not Adam? We know that Jesus suffered real pain. Why not Adam?

Ancient gospel accounts, like the Gospel of Thomas (written at the same time as the canonical ones) that attributed exotic powers to Jesus — as a boy he blessed clay pigeons which then took off in flight — were rejected by the early Church as more fantasy than real. Are we guilty of fantasizing too much about Adam? Should we not defantasize Paradise as they did the gospels?

Consider again our commonly held notions of Adam in Paradise. He suffered no want, no ignorance, no pain. In our parallel are we to ascribe a higher perfection to him than to Jesus? True, all analogies limp, but would not the presumption of a lopsided parallel be weighted more for Jesus who was God/man than for Adam who was just man?

We know that Jesus died a true death. What can we say of Adam? As the earth was filling, could he not possibly choose to die like the rest of creation? After all, it would not have been like our death since he was not guilty of sin.* That death, then, would have allowed him "to pass to the kingdom of God."**

In the light of this possibility, allow me to present a new speculation. Death for sinless Adam would parallel the death of Jesus. Life after death for sinless Adam would parallel the glorified body of Jesus after the resurrection.

To the question, then, would Adam eventually have died had he not sinned, I would answer, given the choice, he would have died the same death as Jesus did. Is there also a corollary here about Eve and Mary?

Reflection

I once asked a congregation, 80 percent of whom had raised their hands to indicate that they had pets at home, how many of them would honestly take their place, if given the chance. Not one hand was raised. Then a child in the third pew sheepishly raised his.

"And a little child shall lead them" (Is 11:6). At that moment that child was closer to Jesus than all the rest of us. We saw the foolishness, the impracticality, and the futility in such a choice. The boy saw only his love for his pet.

St. Paul tells us that Jesus did not consider his equality with God something to grasp at, but that he emptied himself and

---

*It bears mention here that this is not an option for us today because we are all sinners.

**"God put before man life and death, and if he chose life, he was to grow in all virtues and pass to the kingdom of God." Conciliar document of Vatican Council I. Although it was not promulgated, it is considered valuable for its insights.

took the form of a slave (Phil 2:7). Not a son. Not a friend. Not even a pet. But a slave. In doing so, Jesus freely chose to share with us all that becoming human meant—especially death. That is love. That is what we are capable of. That is the love that cannot die, but resurrects unto eternal life.

Prayer

Jesus, help me to be a child. Help me to trust God as a child trusts a parent. Help me to let go of all those things that bind me — my home, my goods, my expectations, my plans, my loves. What is earthbound is bound to remain there. Let my spirit soar with love for the Father and my home, my goods, my expectations, my plans, and my loves will fly with me.

Is It Possible
or Is It Probable?

There's a saying that one tree does not a forest make. Nor does one argument suffice to build a new theory. What I have presented is a series of speculations both scriptural and philosophical to give the reader food for thought. Now I would like to provide a framework in which to consider those speculations.

Consider the difference between the possible and the probable.

While many things may be possible, they are not always probable. Within the realm of speculation, for example, almost anything is possible. It is possible to conceive of a pink elephant with wings. While it is possible (perhaps even through genetic engineering), it is not probable that there will ever be such an animal. In the same way many other things may be considered as possible but not as probable. It is possible to have a tree walk, but it is not very probable that it will ever happen.

Now let us apply this principle to the condition of man in the garden prior to the fall (the original sin). From our earliest religious training we were fed with fantastic representations of life in Eden. We were told that Adam never had pain of any kind — no stomach aches, no headaches, no sore muscles, and so on. Life there was a banquet of exquisite food without effort, recreation without pain, fantasy without end. In short, it was Paradise. It was, as I said before, a sort of original fantasy island. Of course, this is all possible. But is it probable?

There is no question that the evidence of history favors this representation. It would be incongruent with the speculations of most religious thinkers down through the centuries to have had anything but the tamest, most congenial of animals in Paradise. If man did not actually talk to the animals, he most certainly lived in peace with them. One need only recall all the illustrations in catechisms of Adam and Eve in the garden surrounded by a host of wild animals posed peacefully around them. Again, this is possible. But is it probable?

Where did such ideas come from? What is the evidence from scripture itself?

We know from scripture that God is the author of creation and that everything He made was good and even "very good" (Gen 1:31). We know that man was made in the image of God (Gen 1:26) and that God fashioned him out of dust from the soil and breathed into his nostrils the breath of life (Gen 2:7). We know that God gave to man only seed-bearing plants and trees with seed-bearing fruit as his food (Gen 1:29). We know that God placed him in the garden of Eden to cultivate and take care of it (Gen 2:15). Finally, we know that man gave names to all the animals (Gen 2:20).

This is what we know biblically about Paradise. Where did all the rest come from?

The evidence from Genesis is sparse indeed. In the first account of creation, the priestly account, man is made in the image of God (Gen 1:26). This may have given rise to the speculation that man was pain-free, if not fault-free, prior to original sin. After all, it was at the conclusion of His work on the sixth day when He created every kind of living creature (man and beasts) that God saw what He had done was "very good."

However, it was not until "God said, 'See I give you all the seed-bearing plants that are upon the whole earth, and all the trees with seed-bearing fruit; this shall be your food'" (Gen 1:29), that a primitive idyllic life with the animals was probably conceived. Man was not given meat to eat. He was a vegetarian. Therefore, he and the beasts must have dwelt together in peace.

This vision is depicted graphically for us in Isaiah:

The wolf lives with the lamb,
the panther lies down with the kid,
calf and lion cub feed together
with a little boy to lead them.
The cow and the bear make friends,
their young lie down together.
The lion eats straw like the ox.
The infant plays over the cobra's hole;
into the viper's lair
the young puts his hand.
They do no hurt, no harm,
on all my holy mountain,
for the country is filled with the knowledge of Yahweh
as the waters swell the sea. (Is 11:6-9)

It is the vision of the messianic kingdom when all creation will live in harmony. But did that harmony ever exist or is it something that is yet to happen?

In the second account of creation, the Yahwistic account, the tale is more anthropomorphic, more fablelike. "Yahweh God planted a garden in Eden.... (He) caused to spring up from the soil every kind of tree, enticing to look at and good to eat" (Gen 2:8-9). The gold of this land is pure; bdellium and onyx stone are found there (Gen 2:12). The man gave names to all the cattle, all the birds of heaven, and all the wild beasts (Gen 2:20). The man and his wife heard the sound of Yahweh God walking in the garden in the cool of the day (Gen 3:8). Such vivid imagery enhances the impression of peace and harmony between man, God, and creation. But we are left to wonder where all the embellishments came from.

What the ancients had, no less than we, was the obvious manifestations of evil in the world. If what God created was good and if we cannot ascribe evil to God (as the pagans did), where did evil enter the world? The answer was sin; or, more specifically, the sin of Adam. Then, it is a rather simple matter to deduce what life must have been like before sin. One need only posit a state of life opposite to the evils one is experiencing. If there is pain now, there was no pain then. If there are discord, war, and turmoil now, there were peace and harmony then. It was a matter of speculation. It was possible for such a place and time to exist. But was it necessary? Could another possibility exist which also accounts for evil in the world but does not have such an idyllic notion of Paradise?

One biblical scholar, H. Renckens, S.J., solves the problem in a slightly different way. In his book *Israel's Concept of the Beginning*, he claims that, "A world without sin is a purely imaginary world. God created one in which He knew sin would exist."*

In either view there was no magical land of Oz. Can we maintain such a position and still give proper weight to the consequences of sin in the world? Can we maintain such a position and not run afoul of what the scriptures themselves tell us? Is it possible? Is it probable?

*Herder and Herder, 1964, p. 165.

✳ PART III

The Vision:
A New Look
at Paradise

The Way We Were

The day was hot but not all together unpleasant. The man stretched and looked about him. The birds were already chirping noisily about breakfast, which was what woke him up. He glanced over at his mate who was still sleeping peacefully at his side. The rumbling in his stomach told him that they must begin their own morning trek for food.

He woke the woman gently. She stirred lazily and smiled up at him. "I'm hungry," he said simply. "So am I," she replied rising from her comfortable bed.

They moved slowly, neither of them fully awake yet. But once outside and in the direct sunlight their senses came alive to the beauty that surrounded them. The valley below them sparkled with lushness and life. They made their way down a narrow path toward a cluster of heavily laden fruit trees. Momentarily distracted by the antics of some monkeys playing nearby, the woman lost her footing and stumbled. The man hurried instantly to her side.

"Are you all right?"

"I think so."

As he helped her to her feet, she felt a sharp stabbing pain in her left ankle. She winced.

"I think I sprained it," she said as he instinctively grasped her around the waist, supporting her. "How foolish of me not to pay attention to where I was walking."

"Think nothing of it. I will bring us food. Wait here for me. I will return shortly."

He carefully helped her to sit beneath the shelter of a large tree, then hurried out of sight into the brush. She didn't give the incident so much as a second thought. It had happened and it was over. Her husband would return with breakfast. Nothing was lost.

She glanced meditatively at her surroundings. It was something they both did rather often. They enjoyed the full rich beauty of the valley they lived in and the relatively comfortable life it afforded them. Food was plentiful and the living was easy. It was a peaceful place to live. Even the occasional violent thunderstorms did not violate the overriding serenity of it all. If there was anything that marred this Paradise, it would have to be the occasional mishappenstances, like her stumbling, and the mosquitoes. They were an annoyance and in the summertime especially bothersome. But what were these when balanced against so much goodness?

As if reading her thoughts, the pesky insects buzzed busily around her, breaking into her reverie. She waved her hands at them, which seemed, at least temporarily, to hold them at bay. She casually listened to them humming about her, almost mesmerized by their sound. She gave no thought to time, or how long it had been since her husband had left her, or even to her hunger.

It was not uncommon for them to listen to the animals. Not that they understood them, but with the absence of others in the valley they had developed a closeness to them which bordered on communication. It was more like one could imagine what they were saying.

So it was now as she listened to the mosquitoes. They were buzzing about their hunger which reminded her of how hungry she was becoming. Still this did not break her trancelike state. They seemed to be drawing her attention to the tree directly in front of her. The sounds around her changed. The chattering of the monkeys, the singing of the birds, the familiar calls of the other animals all disappeared. The buzzing changed to hissing.

It drew her attention as nothing heretofore ever had. It capti-
vated her, riveted her to the exclusion of everything else. It was
a snake.

She was not startled by it or even frightened by it. It was just
that she had never paid such undivided attention to one. It was
a curious thing. She listened closely to it.

"You are hungry."

"Yes, I am. Come to think of it," she said.

"What are you waiting for? There is fruit aplenty on this tree.
Why not take and eat some?" the snake suggested.

"I am waiting for my husband," the woman replied innocently.

"Why?"

What a strange question, she thought. They had always eaten
together. It had never occurred to her not to.

"He is away getting food for us."

There was a prolonged silence. The woman noticed the sound
of the mosquitoes again and off in the distance the other sounds
of the forest. The snake curled its way back up the limb it was
hanging from and wrapped itself around a particularly succulent
looking fruit. It hissed more loudly than before.

"Has he been gone long?"

"I don't know."

"Ask your stomach."

Her stomach was, in fact, growling more than usual. This was
becoming a very strange encounter indeed.

"There is no need to wait. If you are hungry, eat!"

The woman looked at the fruit. It was indeed pleasant to the
eye and sure to satisfy her hunger. But she had never eaten without her mate. The thought of doing so made her uncomfortable,
like stumbling and spraining her ankle.

The snake saw her consternation. He suggested soothingly,
"Take care of your hunger now. When he returns, he can take
care of his."

The hunger within her seemed more demanding than ever
before. Her husband seemed to have been gone longer than ever

before. She had never thought about any one thing for so long ever before.

"I will," she said, "and I will give my husband some of the fruit when he comes."

The woman hobbled over to the tree and reached up for the fruit the snake had obligingly unwrapped himself from. She took and ate it. When she finished, a mosquito bit her.

"Damn!" she said.

St. Paul's Analogy

"Just as a human body, though it is made up of many parts, is a single unit because all these parts though many, make one body, so it is with Christ. In the one Spirit we were all baptized, Jews as well as Greeks, slaves as well as citizens, and one Spirit was given to us all to drink.

"Nor is the body to be identified with any one of its many parts. If the foot were to say, 'I am not a hand and so I do not belong to the body,' would that mean that it stopped being a part of the body? If the ear were to say, 'I am not an eye, and so I do not belong to the body,' would that mean that it is not a part of the body? The eye cannot say to the hand, 'I do not need you,' nor can the head say to the feet, 'I do not need you.'

"What is more, it is precisely the parts of the body that seem to be the weakest which are the indispensable ones; and it is the least honorable parts of the body that we clothe with the greatest care. So our more improper parts get decorated in a way that our more proper parts do not need. God has arranged the body so that more dignity is given to the parts which are without it, and so that there may not be disagreements inside the body, but that each part may be equally concerned for all the others. If one part is hurt, all parts are hurt with it. If one part is given special honor, all parts enjoy it.

"Now you together are Christ's body."

1 Cor 12:12-27

I Had a Dream

I had a dream. One of those very strange, frustrating dreams. I dreamt that I was ravenously hungry. I searched through the house for something to eat but could find nothing. I wandered out into the back yard and saw a delicious red apple on top of a picnic table. I hurried over to it and reached out to grab it. When my right hand went to grasp it, nothing happened. My fingers just hung there limp and lifeless. I tried again and again, but my hand wouldn't open. I was overcome with panic and frustration, yet I was still curiously hungry. I was pondering this dilemma when suddenly, of itself, my mouth spoke.

"Pick it up," it said to my left hand. I was startled that my mouth should speak without my willing it; but what was stranger still was that it hadn't occurred to me to pick up the apple with my left hand, considering my overwhelming hunger. Yet, the strangest of all was still to follow. I was to become a spectator to all the parts of my body acting quite independently of me.

My left hand simply shrugged, or more precisely, with opened fingers it made a casual gesture as if tossing the suggestion aside.

"I'm hungry," my stomach growled.

"I can't help it," my right hand complained.

"Pick it up!" my mouth ordered the left hand with all the authority it could muster.

There was no response. Somehow, interiorly, I knew that my left hand didn't cooperate because it wouldn't, not because it couldn't. It was certainly a most odd predicament. It was like watching a movie. I was agonizingly frustrated, yet curious about the outcome. And all the time I was getting still hungrier.

With a will of their own, the muscles in my left arm moved the hand toward the desired fruit. It reminded me of the kiddie machines at the amusement park where you control a steam shovel-like scoop to the desired prize only to have it fall and clamp shut over nothing. In my dream, however, the scoop didn't even open . . . it wouldn't open.

"Is there something wrong with you?" my mouth finally asked.

Obstinately quiet, the fingers of my left hand began to move and wiggle, as if demonstrating their dexterity. Then, they curled themselves into a fist. I wasn't sure if it was a gesture of strength or defiance.

"We're waiting," my mouth prodded none too patiently. It was to no avail. My left hand stubbornly refused to cooperate.

"Do something about this." How did I know it was talking to my feet?

Unable to control the actions of my body, I watched it sit on the table and then swing my legs toward the food. I immediately understood that if my hands wouldn't pick it up, my feet were going to. Both feet encompassed the apple and closed in on it. My shoes, however, made the effort impossible. Without my hands to help, my feet scraped against each other in a frustrating attempt to get out of the shoes. Because they were tied, it took a great deal of effort and some scraped ankles before I was successful.

With the apple enclosed in my stocking feet, my legs made a painful attempt to bring the fruit to my mouth. It was an impossible task. No amount of bending and stretching could get me close enough to take a desperately needed bite. The continued efforts exhausted me until I fell back aching and panting.

In a dream, time and circumstances never make much sense so although only moments passed, I knew that I was dying of hunger. I lay weak and helpless on the ground with the apple lying just beyond my reach. I was dangerously close to the final lethargy when no amount of prodding or cajoling would do any good. As if realizing its foolishness, with my mouth too weak to utter a final plea, my left hand slowly inched its way toward the saving fruit. I could feel its smooth skin as my fingers grasped hold of it. I could feel hope stir in my body and my heart quicken in anticipation. In a moment I would be saved.

But the moment didn't come. My left hand was so weakened by my body's hungry state it was unable to lift the prize. It plopped back to the ground with a thud that spelled doom and despair. I could hear myself breathing heavily, suffocatingly.

Now that my left hand was willing to cooperate, it no longer had the strength. Nor did my right hand, if it could have; nor my legs. There was no longer any anger or even hunger — only hopelessness. I turned my head for a last look at the apple. It still lay a few feet away.

Then, from some deep, dormant, indomitable will for survival, my whole body moved in one last desperate attempt. Not my hands, or my arms, or my feet, or my legs, but my whole body in one unified, concerted effort. It rolled over and over until my mouth lay against the apple, my lips touching its savory skin. I bit into it.

Instantly, miraculously, I was restored. I stood up and held the apple between my hands biting into it and relishing every delicious morsel. I was saved.

You Scratch My Back and I'll Scratch Yours

We are all members of one body. The vision that Paul the apostle had was very much like the dream I had. If the eye cannot say to the hand, "I have no need of you," and if one part of the body is in pain, the entire body suffers, then so it is with all of us who are the body of Christ.

This vision that Paul had was a mere microcosm of what was intended by God in creation. There was a oneness, a unity, to all of creation. It came from God; it was all good; as a cosmic unity it is meant to give Him glory. It was created by Him (the Father), through Him (the Son), and for Him (the work of the Holy Spirit). This is the essential oneness that is at the heart of all creation.

This is not to negate the undeniable diversity that exists in creation. There is variety in abundance; in colors, sizes, shapes, types — diversity beyond our limited ability to even imagine. Diversity in the way creation communicates; in the way it increases and multiplies; and in the way it passes on into new forms.

Yet, while this diversity exists, there is a unity. It is like a magnificent symphony written by a master composer. There is variety in the types of instruments played, in the numbers of instruments used, in the notes, chords, and modes that form the composition. But together they form one harmonious, symphonic whole.

Adam and Eve in the garden heard that symphony; they saw it in creation with a clarity that has not been heard or seen since. They knew the essential unity of all that surrounded them. They sensed it. They felt it. They lived in the midst of it. After all, everything around them was good. They saw the ebb and flow of life, the passing days and nights, the changing seasons, birth, life, and death — they saw it all go on around them and they saw that it was good.

They did not know bad. They had not eaten of the fruit of the tree of the knowledge of good and evil. Their focus was entirely on the good things that surrounded them. We can only speculate about what that must have been like.

Like St. Paul's analogy or my dream, there was such a oneness between Adam and Eve that if one of them could not do something that needed to be done, the other did it. Almost without the need to ask. Without the need to say, "thank you." Does the left hand say, "thank you" to the right hand when it picks up a piece of bread? Does the right hand need to say, "thank you" to the mouth for chewing, or the mouth to the stomach for digesting? Such was the vision in the garden before the fall. Man saw only the good. If there were no apple to eat, then he ate a pear. He saw differences, but they were seen as good. An apple tastes good. A pear tastes good. One could even taste better than the other but not that one is worse than the other. It can't be worse since they are both good. There was quantity and there was quality and they were good.

Could Adam have tasted a rotten apple? Yes. But a rotten apple was perceived as something not to eat, not as bad. He merely ate another apple; or if there was none, a pear, or whatever else was handy. It was all in the focus, the state of mind. What Adam had was great equanimity.

Consequently, life around him could have been no different from life as it surrounds us today. There would have been earthquakes and floods, shivering cold, and perspiring heat. Plants and animals would be born, grow, and die. The seasons would come and go and life would proceed in the same way as it does today.

Could Adam have experienced pain? Yes. He could have

sprained his ankle or stubbed his toe or even have lost a hand in an accident. However, such an occurrence would not have been perceived as overwhelming. What one hand couldn't do, the other hand would have to do. If it were something that even the other hand could not do, then Eve would do it. If Eve had an upset stomach, she would wait it out or try home remedies. She would understand that there are some things I can't do today. I will do them tomorrow. If a mosquito bit her where she couldn't scratch it, Adam would.

The Optimist's Prayer

When I was young, my father used to take me to a coffee and doughnut shop that had a very memorable cover on its menu. There were two court jesters, each holding a doughnut, framing a poem called "The Optimist's Prayer." It went like this:

> *As you ramble on through life, brother,*
> *Whatever be your goal,*
> *Keep your eye upon the doughnut,*
> *And not upon the hole.*

In a very real sense this was the vision that Adam and Eve had in the garden before the fall. Their entire focus was on the doughnut, even though they saw the hole and knew that it was there. All of life, all of creation, for them was perceived from that viewpoint. It was all good. They had a global vision. They saw everything as interconnected and interrelated. They were all part of the one. Nothing was perceived as lacking. How could it be? What I do not have, you have and what is yours is mine. Whatever there is, is ours.

This is not such a far-fetched concept. I have a very close friend who's been my friend for years. We grew up together, went to school together, and are priests together. He knows me like a book. One afternoon, he got one of the teen-agers from his parish to wash my car. (The condition it was in was not good.) That evening at dinner, in the midst of ordinary table talk, the thought occurred to me that I would give my ticket to that night's hockey game to the boy in appreciation for what he did. "I just thought of something," I said to him. "Forget it," he said. "You're going to the game with me tonight." I marveled at this because we were not talking about the car or the hockey game. "How did you know?" I asked him. "I know you, John," he laughed.

How many others have experienced similar incidents? Once I was listening to a man describe a dream he had, when his wife, standing next to me, started to laugh. "What's so funny?" I asked. "It was my dream," she said, "not his." Such stories abound if one were to take the time to discover them.

Why, then, could this not have been the constant state of affairs between Adam and Eve before the fall? There was no sin to obscure their vision, no selfishness that would make them see things apart from their interrelatedness. Is that not what sin did to them? To us? We see things dimly now, St. Paul says in his First Letter to the Corinthians (13:12). What must it have been like then?

But even where sin abounds, grace also abounds (Rom 5:21). We are given tastes of what was — what could be — what will be again one day. Our knowledge is still imperfect (1 Cor 13:12). What my priest friend didn't know was that he would end up going to the hockey game with the boy who washed my car.

The Fall

> *"The serpent was the most subtle of all the wild beasts*
> *that Yahweh God had made. It asked the woman,*
> *'Did God really say you were not to eat from any of*
> *the trees in the garden?' The woman answered the*
> *serpent, 'We may eat of the fruit of the trees in the*
> *garden. But of the fruit of the tree in the middle of*
> *the garden God said, "You must not eat it, nor touch*
> *it, under pain of death."' Then the serpent said to*
> *the woman, 'No! You will not die! God knows in fact*
> *that on the day you eat it your eyes will be opened*
> *and you will be like gods knowing good and evil.' The*
> *woman saw that the tree was good to eat and pleasing*
> *to the eye, and that it was desirable for the knowledge*
> *that it could give. So she took some of its fruit and ate*
> *it. She gave some also to her husband who was with*
> *her and he ate it. Then the eyes of both of them were*
> *opened and they realized that they were naked."*
>
> Gen 3:1-7

Since my entire thesis is just a hypothesis, allow me to continue
my speculations. The temptation of Eve was not a temptation to
disobedience. That would have made no sense in the light of her
world. Disobedience was the consequence of the sin. What Eve
saw was good — *it was desirable for the knowledge that it could*
give. An apple is good; a pear is good. Why not this fruit? Eve's
sin was a sin against faith. God said that it was good for her not

to know evil. In the context of all the good that she was aware of, that she had experienced, she should have trusted God's judgment for them.

A sin against faith is a sin against the first commandment. It is putting oneself in the place of God. The serpent's statements were truly subtle. He said, "You will be like gods." He could not have said, "You will become God," for that would have been patently absurd in her eyes. But when he claimed that she would be "like" God, he was inviting her to stand in God's place (before Him) in judgment about what is good for her.

"*Your eyes will be opened,*" the serpent said. The irony of that statement is at the very heart of the sin. In one sense it was true —she would see and know what she did not before. But in another sense, in a far more devastating sense, she would lose her global vision and become myopic. She had chosen not to look at the doughnut but to focus in on the hole. She had narrowed her vision down to what she did not have to the exclusion of all the good that she did have. Henceforth, to be selective and discriminating would mean that she could do so to her detriment. She had lost the vision of interrelatedness, of the unity of all creation in God. It is at the heart of all sin to see things as separate and disconnected. In choosing to eat the fruit, Eve cut herself off. So also do we.

The tree was *in the middle of the garden.* To sin or not to sin was at the very heart of the trial. It is the central point of man's relationship with God. It is the choice between good and evil. One can see himself as intimately related to all of creation knowing that everything one does affects everything else and act for the good of all. Or one can see himself as separate (What I do is my business; this is my body and what I do to it is of no concern to anyone but me) and choose to act accordingly.

"You must not eat it, or touch it *under pain of death.*" This variation in the Jerusalem Bible from the traditional, "lest you die," is interesting indeed. The implied stress here is obviously "the pain" of death. This, too, would be in keeping with the statement of Paul that sin gives death its sting (1 Cor 15:56). It is unquestionable that by nature man is mortal: "For dust you are and to dust you shall return" (Gen 3:19). What then was the consequence of his sin?

Consider what the loss of the universal vision would mean. Man could now focus exclusively on what he doesn't have and not what he has. Differences can be seen as good or bad. You are stronger than I. That is bad. Before, if you were stronger than I and I could not lift this rock, you would. Now, I can see it as having less than you and I am diminished. So, too, with all the rest. You are more intelligent; you are more athletic; you are more beautiful; you are more talented. Consider also the realm of disabilities. You are able to see and I am blind; able to hear and I am deaf; able to walk and I am crippled. When it came to death, Adam must have seen death all around him. Before the fall, he saw it as part and parcel of the ebb and flow of all creation. There is death and there is new life. Now, he could focus in on the negative. It can be seen as separation and isolation and not transition. It can be seen in its finality and awfulness. Before there was immortality—now there can be eternal damnation. Is that the sting of death? Is that the pain of death that eating the forbidden fruit opened his eyes to? Now man can see the other side of God—physical death as the sign of possible eternal death.

✳ *Day Twenty-three*

A Strange Land

Once upon a time there was a very strange land. The people there looked like people everywhere and the homes they lived in looked like those anywhere else. What made it strange was the way the people acted. Day in and day out, all day long the people fought with each other. If they weren't fighting with each other, they would insult one another. If they weren't insulting one another, they would make fun of each other. They spent almost all their time trying to hurt one another any way they could.

You would think that this strange preoccupation made them happy or else why would they do it? But it didn't make them happy. On the contrary, it made them only more miserable than they already were.

One day a good witch chanced upon this strange land. One would hardly expect a witch to be good, but in a land where everything is bad, a good witch is a bad thing.

This good witch decided to cast a spell over the land. She thought and thought and finally decided.

"Roses are red," she said.

"And violets are blue." This spell has a rather classic ring to it, she thought.

"Whatever you say or do,

Will stick like glue—to you!"

With that she sneezed, but no one said *gezundheidt*—that's how bad the place was. "Well," said the good witch, "if someone had, it would have come back a thousand times. Now, I've done my good deed for the day!" Having said that, she left.

Good deed, indeed! No sooner had she departed when the strangest things began to happen. The master of a house, for instance, began to scold a scullery maid. When he did, his tongue stuck to her ear. Well, she would have none of that tomfoolery — no, thank you! After all, what would people think. I mean his tongue being in her ear and all. So she slapped him a mighty blow to the cheek. When she did, her hand stuck there.

At precisely this moment, the mistress of the house entered the room and you can imagine what she thought when she saw her husband's tongue in the scullery maid's ear and her hand on his cheek. This didn't call for thinking but acting, so she gave the two of them a good swift kick. Her foot then stuck to them, causing her to lose her balance, so that she fell on her behind bringing them down with her. At this, she called the maid a most unladylike name. But before she could finish, her tongue stuck in the maid's other ear. Having two tongues in her two ears so infuriated the maid that she swung a mighty blow against the mistress with her other hand. In order to defend herself, the mistress raised her hand so that their two hands stuck together in midair, making them look as if they were dancing. Now the master of the house tried to say something, but with his tongue caught in the scullery maid's ear, all he could do was to murgle. The three of them were caught in a hopeless knot, struggling and murgling against one another!

The commotion brought the butler running. He took one look at the three of them rolling together on the floor, pointed his finger at them, and started laughing. No sooner had a guffaw come out of his mouth, when his finger made a complete about-face and rammed itself into his mouth. Poor butler! Can you imagine how hard it is to talk when you have a finger down your throat? All he could do was to cough and retch.

Elsewhere, similar things were beginning to happen. People everywhere were getting stuck to one another — hands to mouths, feet to hands, and mouths to ears. As if their own plight were not enough, when they encountered others in the same dire straits, they scolded them, "Get out of our way, stupid!" Or they mocked them, "Are you stuck on one another?" Or they ridiculed them, "Are you two going around together?" No sooner was the nasty remark made when one group would stick to another group. Before long, groups were stuck to one another in an almost endless chain. They all had to move or roll together if they wanted to go anywhere. And, if they complained, their tongues too became stuck so that nothing they said made any sense.

Mind you, all of this was happening because of the good witch's spell. It was lucky for them that a bad wizard happened to come along.

"What have we here?" he cried. "It breaks me up to see you all so attached to one another." The people tried to say something, but all they could do was to murgle.

"That good-for-nothing good witch did this to you. Unfortunately, one witch cannot break the spell of another witch. All I can do is to change it somewhat. This calls for devilishly clever ingenuity. Let me think!" muttered the wizard.

"Yes! I have it! Perfect! Just what the doctor ordered."

He then raised his arms and cast his own counter-spell:

> *"Give them ears that do not hear.*
> *Give them eyes that do not see.*
> *Then, their will they still will bear.*
> *But of the spell, they are not free!"*

No sooner had he finished the incantation, when everyone broke free from everyone else. They all got up and brushed themselves off. They were about to thank the bad wizard, which would have been a good thing—but then would he really have been a bad wizard? After all, did he not do a good thing by setting all these people free? Or did he?

Anyway, they were about to thank him when the mistress of the house let loose a mighty barrage of invective—that's the polite way of saying nasty things—against her husband and the scullery maid who started all of this in the first place. At that instant, she remembered the spell and clapped her hands against her mouth. She looked around cautiously, then slowly took her hands away, half expecting her tongue to stick somewhere. But it didn't happen. As a matter of fact, nothing happened. It would have felt wonderful except she hadn't finished scolding the two of them. When they saw that nothing happened to her, they picked up right where they left off, bickering and quarreling. Even the butler got his two cents in. In no time at all, everything was back to normal again.

Or was it? Was the good witch bad or the bad wizard good? The spell was not broken, only changed.

> *Give them ears that do not hear.*
> *Give them eyes that do not see.*
> *Then, their will they still will bear.*
> *But of the spell, they are not free.*

"Fortunately!" said the good witch.

"We shall see," said the bad wizard.

It was indeed a strange land. But, lest the reader be in doubt, the moral of the story is, "We're really better off when we're stuck together."

✳ PART IV

The Vision Restored

✳ *Day Twenty-four*

I Have Often Walked on This Street Before

If my hypothesis is correct, the conclusion is inevitable that the cosmos, the earth, the garden of Eden are no different now from the way they were then (excluding, of course, the gift of immortality). It is the same world with the same possibilities and the same probabilities. There was no magical land of Oz before or now.

If that's the case, then what was the difference between life before the fall and life after the fall? What made the garden of Eden Paradise?

The only thing that changed was man — not the world that surrounded him. That world remained constant, functioning according to the nature that God had given it. It was man that changed — that was the difference. He was not the same after sin as before it. Sin had immutably affected his outlook on life. His perspective had gone from global to particular. He went from magnanimity to selfishness and that myopic self-centeredness would be passed on by him to all future generations. It was his legacy — the stain of original sin.

If it had been otherwise, if the garden of Eden had been a magical land free of pain and suffering, if all pain and suffering were the result of sin, how do we account for the statement of Jesus about the man born blind? How do we make an accounting for the innumerable people who suffer sickness and disability who are innocent of sin: children born handicapped, whole populations indiscriminately wiped out by plague, millions of people disfigured and maimed because of accidents? Can we say that all these people are guilty of the kinds of sins that would demand such a heavy recompense? Are we not forced to make this God of love an ogre?

On the other hand, if we say that the world God created was good, then it could be made better. If we say that life wasn't a bowl of cherries, then Adam had to work and till the ground for his sustenance. If we say there could have been handicapping conditions before the fall, then we are not forced into the position that God arbitrarily, if not whimsically, imposed incredible hardships and handicapping conditions on certain of His children so that His glory may be made manifest. What does that do to His justice? Is the punishment commensurate with the crime? How can we ever answer the question, "Why me, God?"

If the world before the fall was no different, and only man changed, then we can recapture Paradise if we regain what he lost. It was Adam's vision that made Eden Paradise. If we had that vision today, then we would realize that the kingdom of heaven is now. Paradise surrounds us. If only we had the eyes to see it. One can enter the kingdom without waiting for the second coming of Jesus. The miracle of Paradise is available to the lame and the halt, the young and the old—and it's available right now!

In the musical *My Fair Lady*, Freddie sings, "I have often walked on this street before. But the pavement always stayed beneath my feet before." It was the same street he had trod countless times before. What made the difference? He was in love. It altered his whole outlook on the ordinary. He was elevated above the commonplace. When you are in love, all is well with the world.

When one comes out of his own self-centeredness to love another, one gets a taste of the vision. Paradise is open to all, right here and now. But is a taste enough? How can we permanently restore the vision?

To Dream
the Impossible Dream

"So Yahweh God expelled him from the garden of Eden to till the soil from which he had been taken. He banished the man, and in front of the garden of Eden he posted the cherubs, and the flame of a flashing sword, to guard the way to the tree of life" (Gen 3: 23,24).

God had offered man the option to choose life and live or to choose death and die. Adam opted for death. The way back to paradise was blocked. Man would have to grope in the darkness he had willed upon himself. The situation should have been hopeless. But God said to the devil:

> *"I will make you enemies of each other:*
> *you and the woman,*
> *your offspring and her offspring.*
> *It will crush your head*
> *and you will strike its heel."* (Gen 3:15)

There was the promise of someone who would crush the power of Satan. However, he would have to pay the price. There was a way back. It was promised. It is the only way. Jesus is the way back. He is the way and the truth and the life. In Jesus the vision is restored. To those who hold fast to Jesus, the kingdom of heaven is at hand. Paradise is now.

In the incarnation, God invades humanity in a new way, in a

restorative way. Humanity is radically saved by the second Adam as it was radically disoriented by the first Adam. All things were made by God, through the Son, for the glory of God. When man was given dominion over creation, he was meant to order all things for the glory of God. Through sin, he could manipulate it for his own glory. Through restored humanity, creation is restored. How was this worked out in time?

While anticipating the coming of the savior, the children of Adam were not left to despair and damnation. God was constantly calling them back through covenant to restore the relationship. Sin had so disoriented him that man would hold the vision for a while and then he let it slip through his fingers once again. It was no longer a constant state but one that would have to be affirmed through faith expressed in repeated acts of love. St. John said it in his first epistle: "God is love, and he who abides in love, abides in God and God in him" (1 Jn 16). It is impossible to love apart from God. Whenever someone loves, God is present. The more man opens himself to love, the greater is his possession of the kingdom of God.

All humanity was affected by the incarnation, before as well as after Jesus, since the action of God is timeless. Even Adam had to be saved by Christ. Original sin predates Jesus only in human terms, according to man's time. But God's action encompasses all time. The fall and the incarnation are simultaneous to God. God's mercy and restoration through Jesus were present at the moment of the fall. It was only in time that man would come to understand the truth of it.

I Wouldn't Have It Any Other Way

When Jean Vanier, a wonderful, charismatic worker among the mentally and physically handicapped, was asked on a Paris television program how a severely handicapped girl felt about her situation, he let her answer for herself. Her only form of communication was a typewriter which she laboriously worked at for her reply. Her response was, "I wouldn't have it any other way." She had given her life to Christ. She has the vision.

If I were to put on sunglasses and stand next to someone who was not wearing them, we would both see the same thing. Only I would see it differently. When we do as St. Paul said and put on Christ, we see life differently. We see life through "Jesus glasses." We see all things working together for good. We see the interrelatedness of all creation in the will of God. We see that everything that God makes is good. We see that there is a purpose for everything under the sun.

No life is meaningless. No human life is less because of its physical or mental condition. There is only good that can be made better when we till the soil. Inferior, lacking, disabled, and so on, are not words of the kingdom. We are all members of one body and the body is Christ.

The innocent blind man is given sight by Jesus so that *we* might see. "Go back and tell John what you hear and see; the blind see again, and the lame walk, lepers are cleansed, and the deaf hear, and the dead are raised to life and the Good News is proclaimed to the poor; and happy is the man who does not lose faith in me" (Mt 11:4-5). Jesus has fulfilled the prophecies. He has done the works that would point him out as the long-awaited Messiah. The healings were the signs.

Signs are meant to point. They are not meant as ends in themselves. We are not supposed to get lost in the signs, in the healings. They are intended to direct you somewhere — to someone. The works are meant to lead us to Jesus. Time and again he tells his listeners, "If you refuse to believe in me, at least believe in the works I do" (Jn 10:38; 5:36; 14:11). Belief in Jesus is more important than the works. Why?

At Bethany, Judas reproves Christ for allowing the sinful woman to squander precious ointment on his feet. It should be sold and the money given to the poor. Jesus replies, "Leave her alone. . . . The poor you have always with you" (Jn 12:8). Judas did not have the vision. He would get lost in the works and fail to see that their purpose is only to lead to Jesus. If one has Jesus, what need is there for the works?

Jesus could well have said, "The sick and the disabled, you have always with you." If they possess Jesus, what need have they of healings? The healings are certainly good. To be healed of blindness is even a greater good. However, to possess Jesus is the greatest good. That gives one a vision of life that has no need of eyesight. Indeed, one could then enter the kingdom of heaven less an eye or a hand and still not be diminished; one could enter the kingdom of heaven where there will be no marrying nor giving in marriage and not feel a loss. How else can we understand why Jesus would leave so many sick people at the pool of Bethzatha?

Consider, if you will, that all the people Jesus healed got sick again! It is a fact. I utter no blasphemy. I do Jesus no disservice. Jesus himself said to the paralytic he cured at the pool, "Go and sin no more, lest something worse befall you" (Jn 5:14). I'm sure that the lepers he cleansed did not spend the rest of their lives free from all illness. The deaf man could very likely have gotten crippling arthritis. The man with the withered hand could have gotten leprosy. Lazarus himself is most assuredly dead, or he would certainly stink by now.

If we get lost in the signs, then we are trapped in a snare of our own making. If the presence of the kingdom of God were dependent upon the signs, Jesus would have to be constantly at our beck and call. He would have to cure us of a headache today, a fever tomorrow, depression the day after. We will have made the body perfect, our God. It is a subtle trap. Remember that the serpent was the most subtle of all the wild beasts.

If my hypothesis serves no other purpose than to point out the primacy of Jesus over all things, including healings, then it will have served its purpose.

✳ *Day Twenty-seven*

What Is Good?

When one has the vision of life that is restored in Jesus, one's outlook radically changes. When seen through the eyes of Jesus, then good, g-o-o-d, is perceived as an extension of God, G-o-d. Consequently, all the good in the world is somehow related to the action of God. Man cannot perform good apart from God. Therefore, the good of the kingdom is already taking place wherever good things are happening. This is not a metaphor but theological truth. God is healing the sick in a myriad of ways. The blind are given sight, the deaf have their hearing restored to them, lepers are cleansed, and the poor are having the Good News preached to them. Those who have not yet heard the Good News of Jesus are no more excluded than those who predated his incarnation. They enter into the action of God through love and their good works (1 Jn 16).

But the situation is not final. There is still sin in the world. The totality of the kingdom is not yet present. It is under siege now, as it was in the time of Christ. The work of the Adversary continues. We must bear in mind that the Good News of Jesus is more important than all the miracles. If ultimate pain and death have been conquered by Jesus, then what matter the lesser deaths? What matter the lesser deaths of arthritis, lumbago, muscular dystrophy, cancer? Death has been swallowed up in victory. "O death! Where now is your victory? Where is your sting?" (1 Cor 15:55). But that vision is only for those who have the eyes of faith to see it.

Whose Cross Is It, Anyway?

Man lives his life from minute to minute. Not so God. There is no past or future in God. His action is now—eternally now.

As God/man Jesus' actions are both temporal and eternal. While we cannot fathom the mystery, we can appreciate the benefits of that union. As much as the incarnation was present in the garden of Eden, so also was the crucifixion: "And you will strike its heel." The price for mankind's sin was paid once and for all. As Son of God, Jesus' crucifixion was eternal. It is present to all time.

Because we are bound up in man's time, we enter into the saving death of Jesus minute by minute. In a commentary on Psalm 85, St. Augustine explains it this way: "God could give no greater gift to men than to make his Word, through whom he created all things, their head and to join them to him as his members, so that the Word might be both Son of God and son of man, one God with the Father, and one man with all men. Let us then recognize both our voice in his, and his voice in ours." We might also add, our cross in his, and his cross in ours.

St. Paul says, "In my own flesh I make up what is lacking in the sufferings of Christ for the sake of his body, the Church" (Col 1:24). What could possibly be lacking in that ignominious suffering and death that Christ endured? What, but for that to be worked out in time. Christ waits for us to live out his/our suffering in time.

Jesus is dying on the cross this very minute! This is not by way of analogy. This is not mystical poetry. It is theological fact.

Our sins are crucifying him at this very moment. He is bearing the weight of all sins from the time of Adam to the last man, since as son of God he is present to all of human history. "Before Abraham came to be, I am" (Jn 8:58).

If we enter into Jesus through faith, our sufferings take on a new perspective. We share the burden with him and our pain becomes salvific. He shares the burden with us and with it comes the promise of future glory. Through the cross we share the cost that was paid for the sins of all mankind. Adam lost the gift of immortality and so all men must die. Jesus restores the gift but only through his passion, death, and resurrection. Suffering makes sense only when we join it to the saving work of Jesus. Apart from Jesus, it is a problem without a solution.

When we share the global vision, we see beyond a doubt the eternal truth in the words of Jesus, "I tell you solemnly, in so far as you did this to one of the least of these brothers of mine, you did it to me" (Mt 25:40).

In our terms, it is as if Jesus sees that the burden we are carrying is too heavy for us and we shall most surely be crushed to death. We could not bear the full intensity of our cancer, our muscular dystrophy, our deafness, our grief, so he accepts it on the cross. But such a heavy burden is almost too much for him to bear since he is not only God but man. Therefore, we help him by sharing the load.

In God's terms, the action is all one. He is the head and we are members of his body, and the whole body works together for the good of all. "There are no more distinctions between Jew and Greek, slave and free, male and female, but all of you are one in Christ Jesus" (Gal 3:28). It is the will of Jesus that all his actions are done for our sake. We must make it our will to join him if life, suffering, and death are to make sense.

The Pushcart

Once upon a time, there was a man plodding down a country road. He strained mightily against the weight of a cart heavily laden with bricks. The task was almost too much for him to bear. From seemingly out of nowhere, a stranger appeared and offered to relieve him of his load. This was indeed strange, not just because no one had ever offered to help him before, but because the stranger's cart was more full than his own. Unlike his own cart neatly stacked with rectangular, red bricks, the stranger's cart was filled with bricks and stones of every size, shape, and color. Too grateful to object, the man watched as the stranger emptied his cart of all its bricks.

Relieved of his burden, the light-hearted man continued on his journey, the cart bouncing happily behind him. He came upon an inn where he indulged himself in a fine supper and a night of well-deserved rest.

The next morning when he went out to resume his journey, he was met by the stranger who had just arrived at the inn.

"I need your help in order for me to continue on," he said.

Reluctantly, he agreed to take back some of his bricks. When the stranger indiscriminately removed not just his own red, rectangular bricks, but whatever bricks and stones came into his reach, the man objected most strenuously.

"These are not all mine!" he protested.

"No matter," exclaimed the stranger. "I cannot tarry here any longer. If you wish, you may return those that are not yours to their proper owners who will surely be passing along this way."

Rather than continue his journey with a burden that was not rightly his, the man decided to wait and do as the stranger suggested. He did not have to wait long. In the distance he saw a cart approaching with its load of yellow bricks gleaming in the sunlight.

"Now I can rid myself of these yellow bricks."

When the cart drew close to him and he finally took his attention off the bricks, he saw that it was being dragged along by a very old and weary man. He remembered his own struggle of the day before and knew that he would not have the heart to add to the poor man's burden. As it was, the old man could barely manage the load he was hauling. Instead, the man took a few more yellow bricks off the cart as it bumped along past him.

"No matter. I have plenty of others here that I can get rid of."

Soon another cart approached. This one was filled with big grey stones. Here, at last, was the opportunity to get rid of some of the big grey ones that lay heavily on his load.

Again, when the cart neared, his attention was drawn from the load to the one pushing it. This one was preceded by a crippled boy.

"Such an awful burden for one so young and disabled!" he cried.

Once again, instead of unloading some of his cart, he removed stones from the crippled boy's cart. Somewhat exasperated, he sat down to wait for another arrival.

The next cart was pushed along by a blind woman and the following by a sickly man. Again and again, he relieved the passers-by of some of their load instead of giving them that part of his which was rightly theirs.

As evening drew on, he decided to wait no longer, for in fact he had succeeded only in adding to his own load. When he looked at his cart, he should not have been startled to find it filled to overflowing with bricks and stones of different colors and sizes.

"What else could I do?" he muttered as he positioned himself between the cart's extended arms. He gave a mighty tug. The cart would not budge. He braced himself, gathered all his strength, and tried again. Finally, it began to move. He inched along down the dirt road once more.

"Strange," the man thought, "but it doesn't seem heavy at all."

Much Ado About Something

A famous healer was once asked, "Why are some people healed and not others?" The reply given was one that has echoed down through the centuries, "I don't know."

No answer has ever really been satisfactory. The customary ones are: the proper faith was lacking; sin has prevented the healing. Either of these conditions could be attributed to the sick person or the healer or any combination of both.

But I have seen nonbelievers healed as well as public sinners. Where does that leave the innocent and the faithful?

In struggling through this dilemma, I reached the conclusion that if Paradise were suffering-free and sin were the only reason for pain, then those innocent of sin were specifically chosen for sickness, disability, and misfortune, for God knows what reason. Consequently, "Why me, God?" could never be answered reasonably or hopefully. This God of love would be a difficult, if not impossible, pill to swallow.

But if the parallel between then and now, between life in the garden of Eden and today, were not so diametrically different, then:

- life and creation was good then and is now;
- life and creation could be made better then as well as now;
- sickness and suffering need not be any more overwhelming now than it was then;
- nature, while good, was not perfect and, therefore, there could have been "disabilities" and "imperfections" (only in retrospect) then as there are now;

• God didn't choose me specifically to suffer with no accountable reason for it;

• it was the "vision of oneness" that was lost through original sin;

• it was out of divine condescension that God sent Jesus to restore that vision;

• while miracles and healings are better than sickness and disability, there is something better yet than even these, namely, Jesus;

• these "signs" are given as a taste of what can be, so that we hunger for the whole meal and are not content with just the appetizers;

• most importantly, Paradise (the kingdom of God) is as possible and probable now, as it was then — through Jesus.

Yet, with all this, I still don't know why this person with cancer was healed and not that person with muscular dystrophy, any more than I know why Jesus picked the one paralytic at the pool of Bethzatha over all the others. I can only say that for me there is greater light and hope in a theory that calls for mosquitoes in Paradise than in one that ignores them.

✳ PART V

The Solution

The Parable

Once upon a time a man was told that he had an incurable illness. The news filled him with great sadness for he had dreamed dreams and hoped hopes, and now it seemed that they would never come true. One day he heard that there was a wizard who could do wonderful things for people, so he decided to visit him.

"What is it you want?" asked the wizard.

"I have dreamed dreams and hoped hopes," replied the man.

"What have you dreamed?"

"I have dreamed of a home, a home of my own to live in — a big home with many rooms and fine furniture."

"You have but to ask," said the wizard.

With that, he snapped his fingers and at once, in the twinkling of an eye, there stood a beautiful home. Nay, not a home, a palace — not even a palace, a castle. The castle was far bigger, far more beautiful than any he had ever dreamed of. There were almost too many rooms to count, and each one was filled with exquisite furniture. The man was filled with joy as he entered his house, walked its halls, and explored its rooms.

But then, in time, he remembered the illness and again was filled with sadness. He returned to the wizard.

"What is it you want of me?" asked the wizard.

"I have dreamed dreams and I have hoped hopes," the man replied.

"The Parable" first appeared in *Story Sunday* (copyright 1978 by the Missionary Society of St. Paul the Apostle in the State of New York) and is reprinted by permission of Paulist Press.

"What have you dreamed?"

"I have dreamed of food, food fit for a king. Food that would fill all my cravings, food as I have never eaten before."

"You have but to ask," said the wizard.

And he snapped his fingers. At once, in the twinkling of an eye, the castle table was covered with fine and delicious food. Never had the man seen such food or tasted such goodness. It was food fit for a hundred kings. He was filled with joy as he sat at the banquet table.

But then, in time, he remembered the sickness and the sadness came over him again. He returned to the wizard.

"What is it you want of me?" asked the wizard.

"I have dreamed dreams and I have hoped hopes," said the man.

"Tell me what have you dreamed."

"I have dreamed of clothes—fine, rich and beautiful clothes."

"You have but to ask," said the wizard.

Once again he snapped his fingers and at once the man was clothed in the finest clothes he had ever seen. His castle was filled with clothes, rich and beautiful clothes of the finest cloth imaginable. So the man walked his castle in his exquisite clothes, and sat at table to the finest of foods, and he was filled with happiness.

But then, in time, he remembered the incurable sickness, and a great sorrow overcame him.

"Why are you still sad?" asked the wizard. "Have I not fulfilled your dreams and hopes? Do you not have a castle, and clothes and food just as you wished? Why, then, are you still sad?"

"Because I have an incurable illness," the man cried.

"I can cure that," said the wizard.

The man's face quickly changed to hope.

"You can cure that!" he exclaimed. "Why, if you can cure that, what do I care about the rest? If you can cure the sickness, I don't care where I live or what I eat or what I wear. None of that really matters if you can cure my sickness."

"You have but to ask," replied the wizard.

He then snapped his fingers, and in an instant, in the twinkling of an eye, the man was cured of his illness.

So the man walked away—away from the castle, away from the delicious food, away from the exquisite clothes. He walked away from all of them—filled with joy, happier than he had ever been in his entire life.

What does this parable mean? Life is a terminal illness. When man first realized that life would come to end, when he saw the grass die, and the leaves die, and the trees die, and animals die, and his companions die, and he knew that one day he, too, would die, he was filled with great sadness.

One day he learned of a great wizard, a wonder-worker—God. So man went before his God.

"What is it you want of me?" God asked.

"I have dreamed dreams and I have hoped hopes," replied man.

"Tell me, what is it you've dreamed?" asked the Lord God.

"I have dreamt of a house, a fine and luxurious house for me to live in," replied the man.

"You have but to ask," said God, and He snapped His fingers, and at once man had a place to live. A home of deep, rich earth with a mossy, green carpet, a home lit by the sun during the day, and the moon and stars at night. And man made his home— homes of mud and mortar, homes of brick and stone, homes of wood and glass and steel, ranch homes and split levels, homes of one story and homes that reached into the sky.

Man was filled with joy over his home, and he walked its halls with great delight. But then, in time, he remembered he would die, and a great sadness overcame him. So he went back to God.

"What is it you want of me?" asked the Lord.

"Lord, I have dreamed dreams and I have hoped hopes!"

"Tell me what you have dreamed."

"I've dreamed of food, food to fill my every yearning, food to satisfy my every hunger."

"You have but to ask," said the Lord God, and He snapped His fingers, and in an instant there was spread before man a banquet of food, far beyond his dreams. Food from the earth was there: green vegetables and fruits of infinite variety. There was food from the seas—fish of every variety and shape: lobster, crab, shrimp, scallops, pike, trout, and bass. Food from the land was there: beef, lamb, venison, and pork. There was, in fact, every kind of meat. Food from the heavens was there: duck, geese, quail, and pheasant. The man's banquet table was filled beyond his wildest imagining. So he ate and his heart was full of joy. But then, in time, he remembered he would die, and his sorrow returned. Again, he went to his God.

"What is it you want of me?" asked God.

"I have dreamed dreams and hoped hopes," sighed the man.

"What have you dreamed?"

"I have dreamed of clothes—fine, rich, and exquisite clothes. Clothes fit for a king!"

"You have but to ask," said the Lord, and again, He snapped His fingers. In an instant the man was clothed in magnificent attire. Clothes of wool, silk, velvet, and cotton. Clothes of every size, shape, color, and fabric. Warm clothes for winter and light clothes for summer. Clothes for morning, noon, and night. Clothes fit for a hundred kings. So the man wore the clothes, and walked his castle, and ate his fill and in his heart, there was joy.

But then, once again, he remembered he must die. Again, a great sadness overwhelmed him.

"Why are you still sad?" asked God.

"Because I must die," man cried.

"I can cure that," said God.

"You can cure that? You can cure death? Why, if you can cure death, then I really don't care where I live, or what I eat, or what I wear. None of that matters if you can cure death!"

"You have but to ask," said God.

With that, the Lord God snapped His fingers, and in an instant, in the twinkling of an infinite eye . . . *there was Jesus!*

And the man walked away. Away from the food, and the exquisite clothes. The man walked away from all of them as if they
were nothing. Cured of death, he walked away, his heart filled
with joy—happier than in any dream he had ever dreamt, happier than he'd ever hoped, happier than he had ever been in his
entire life.

Reflection

During the writing of this manuscript I was called to the hospital about an emergency admission. A healthy, happy, and
bright thirteen-year-old girl had suffered an embolism in the
brain. Her parents, recent friends of mine, had only within the
last year come to a renewal of their faith and were actively in-
volved in bringing that experience to others. My heart sank
when I entered the Intensive Care Unit and saw a flat EEG. She
looked so young and helpless lying there amid the tubes and
wires that protruded everywhere from her stricken body. One
look at the nurse told all.

I took her limp hand in mind and prayed with all the fervor
and faith that was within me. "Why, Lord? Why? She is so young,
so vibrant! Yet, even now I know that if you willed it, she could
rise from this bed fully restored, fully alive. Will it, Lord.
Please, will it!" I prayed silently because I did not want her father
who stood beside me to hear my pleading and my questioning. I
did not want my faltering faith to weaken his, so newly enliv-
ened. What a test for these good parents to have to undergo so
soon after their rebirth. "Why must the good suffer, Lord? I
wish evil on no man, but certainly there are others more deserv-
ing of this fate than this innocent child."

There was a week of parish renewal going on at their church
and her mother and father were leading it when she was stricken.

"Lord, how will this win others to you? How in the midst of their doing such good can such a terrible evil happen? Were you sleeping, Lord, as you were in the boat on the sea of Galiliee? Wake up! We are sinking. Calm the storm. Heal the child."

I lost all sense of time. I envisioned Jesus saying, "The child is not dead. She is asleep." Wouldn't that be wonderful! I thought of the wonderment of the doctors and nurses at the miracle. No doubt they would explain it away in some abstruse medical jargon. But I would know. We would know. We'd let the whole world know. I left the hospital with an uplifted spirit.

The next night was my turn to speak at the parish renewal. Because of a busy schedule I was unable to contact anyone about the state of the child, but I wasn't worried. My evening meditation had yielded the consolation, "What I have in mind for her is greater than what all of you can imagine or hope for."

I was met with the news, "Michelle died."

"Oh, God, help me!" My first thought was of myself. How typical! My countenance must have betrayed my thoughts for I was told in the next instant that her parents were taking the loss wonderfully well. Somewhere in the mix of the emotions of that confused time I thanked God for their courage and faith; I prayed about my disappointment; I begged for help in the talk I was about to give.

It was at the coffee social afterward that the devastating blow came. What I feared, yet what I knew was inevitable, was finally voiced. A group of men cornered me. Michelle's parents had stopped by on their way home to thank the community for their love and support. "God's will be done," they said and everyone knew they meant it. Now, as one of the group recalled it, an irate father shouted, "That's a lot of bull!" Everyone in the small hall heard it. All eyes turned toward us. I felt my face flush crimson.

"Oh, God. It is so easy to believe when all is going well." I remembered reading somewhere that "lead us not into temptation" could also be translated, "do not put us to the test." "Lord, let me talk about you when the sun is shining, when there are rainbows sparkling brilliantly in the sky and the earth is filled with sweetness. Please, don't put me to the test. Not here. Not now."

How can you say in a few words what even the faltering words of this lengthy manuscript cannot say adequately? How can you say that the deceiver has done his job well; that we value this life more than the next; that it is the Spirit that God breathed into us that makes us great and not this paltry body; that faith is a gift freely given but severely tested only by fire; that death has been swallowed up in victory; that eye has not seen nor ear heard nor can the mind of man imagine all that God has prepared for those who love Him?

"Oh God. Do not put me to the test!"

Prayer

Lord, I believe. Help my unbelief!